The Bible Pageant Series

—»»-»»-»» «« «« ««—

BRAVE PIONEERS

CONQUERING HEROES

KINGS AND QUEENS

THE MIGHTY PRINCE

WARRIORS OF THE CROSS

THE BIBLE PAGEANT

Volume One

BRAVE PIONEERS

The Bible Pageant

by MERLIN L. NEFF, Ph.D.

VOLUME ONE

BRAVE PIONEERS

Scripture in the Stories From J. M. Powis Smith and
Edgar J. Goodspeed, The Bible, an American Translation

PACIFIC PRESS PUBLISHING ASSN., Mountain View, California
Brookfield, Illinois   Cristobal, Canal Zone   Omaha, Nebraska
Portland, Oregon

"THEY WERE STRANGERS AND PILGRIMS ON THE EARTH."

EXPLANATION

Wherever conversation is employed in the Bible stories, the words of the characters are taken directly from the Scriptures. However, the language of *The Bible, an American Translation,* by J. M. Powis Smith and Edgar J. Goodspeed, is the translation used, with the kind permission of the University of Chicago Press. This translation offers the young readers modern language that is easily understood without in any way marring the beauty or inspiration of the word.

Library of Congress
Catalog Card Number 47-20254

Seventh Printing

1954

PACIFIC
PRESS
PUB.
ASSN.

PRINTED
IN U·S·A·

DEDICATION

To my wife and son, who love the stories of the Book of books, and who encouraged me in writing these volumes for the youth of today, THE BIBLE PAGEANT is humbly dedicated.

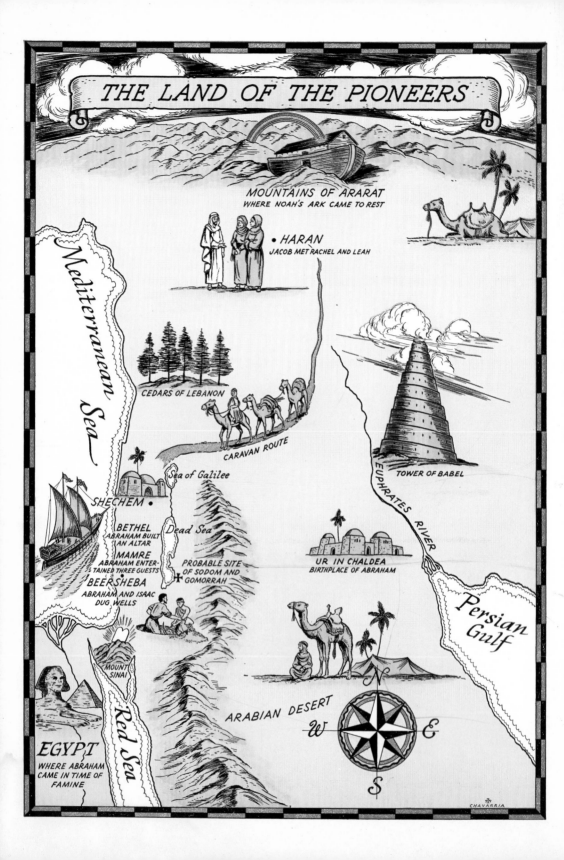

THE LAND OF THE PIONEERS

MOUNTAINS OF ARARAT
WHERE NOAH'S ARK CAME TO REST

• HARAN
JACOB MET RACHEL AND LEAH

Mediterranean Sea

CEDARS OF LEBANON

CARAVAN ROUTE

TOWER OF BABEL

Sea of Galilee

SHECHEM •

BETHEL
ABRAHAM BUILT
AN ALTAR

MAMRE
ABRAHAM ENTER-
TAINED THREE GUESTS

BEERSHEBA
ABRAHAM AND ISAAC
DUG WELLS

Dead Sea

PROBABLE SITE
OF SODOM AND
GOMORRAH

UR IN CHALDEA
BIRTHPLACE OF ABRAHAM

EUPHRATES RIVER

Persian Gulf

MOUNT
SINAI

ARABIAN DESERT

EGYPT
WHERE ABRAHAM
CAME IN TIME OF
FAMINE

Red Sea

N
W E
S

CHAVARRIA

CONTENTS

STORY CHAPTER I:

   THE BOOK OF BOOKS 11

STORY CHAPTER II:

   WHO TOLD THE BATS AND THE SQUIRRELS? 24

     1. A World Is Made 43

     2. An Enemy in the Garden 55

     3. When Cain Hated His Brother 63

     4. The Flood Destroys the Earth 69

     5. Building the First City 81

      (Captain Tim's Bible Quiz, Number 1) 85

STORY CHAPTER III:

   BURIED CITIES AND STRANGE WRITING 87

     6. A Selfish Choice and a Kidnaping 97

     7. Three Visitors on a Strange Mission 105

     8. Abraham's Two Sons 113

     9. Abraham's Greatest Test 117

     10. The Search for a Bride 123

STORY CHAPTER IV:

   QUEER CUSTOMS OF LONG AGO 135

     11. The Adventures of Twin Boys 147

     12. Jacob Flees for His Life 155

     13. A Fight in the Dark 165

      (Captain Tim's Bible Quiz, Number 2) 173

STORY CHAPTER V:

    FROM DAN TO BEERSHEBA 174

        14. Joseph the Dreamer 187

        15. A Slave in Prison 195

        16. From Prison to Palace 201

        17. Food for the Hungry 209

STORY CHAPTER VI:

    THE LAND OF THE PYRAMIDS 217

        18. Joseph Faces His Brothers 233

        19. Father and Son Meet 243

        20. Under a Cruel King 247

        (Captain Tim's Bible Quiz, Number 3) 250

PREFACE

In presenting the living story of the Bible for boys and girls, it is the sincere purpose of the author to transfer youth from this modern world into the life and experiences of Old Testament men and women. If the Bible is to be loved by youth, it must be read and understood by them. They must find the thrill of adventuring in the Eternal Book. The loves, the hopes, the fears, the faith of those who loved God make the eternal story that has been reverently cherished by a hundred generations.

Wherever conversation is employed in these Bible stories, the words of the characters are taken directly from the Scriptures. However, *The Bible, an American Translation,* by J. M. Powis Smith and Edgar J. Goodspeed, is the translation used, with the kind permission of The University of Chicago Press. This translation offers the young readers modern language that is easily understood without in any way marring the beauty or inspiration of the word.

The story chapters are planned to lead youth into the Bible and to enrich the Scriptures with valuable facts about the country, the people, the history, the natural science, and the human interest elements that are closely linked with the Book of books.

May this volume have such an influence upon the ideals and character of youth that they will be constrained to love the Bible, follow its precepts, and allow its influence to mold their lives and their destiny.

THE AUTHOR.

The BOOK of Books

THREE figures moved quietly along the walk by the side of the Lane house. They stopped at the basement window and listened for any sounds. Then they made their way to the gate opening into the back yard. Dick Barrett, thirteen years old and tall for his age, lifted the latch, and the squeaky gate swung back on its hinges. The twins, Bette and Roy, who were two years younger than their brother, entered the yard first and surveyed it carefully.

"I suppose we should see if he is here," said Bette.

"Of course," replied Dick. "It is part of our job."

"If he isn't here, why did we see a light in the house last night?" queried Roy.

"Look," said Bette, pointing to the basement door. "It's open."

"Hello, Captain Tim! Are you home?" Dick called, walking down the steps and peering in at the open door.

"Hello, indeed! Yes, I'm here at my workbench," came the response.

"That sounds good to me," admitted Bette to her brothers. "I was worried for a minute."

"What for?" asked Dick. "There certainly wasn't anything to be scared about."

(11)

"Who's scared?" greeted the captain, coming to the door and smiling at his three friends.

W. WILKE, ARTIST

"Who's scared?" greeted the man, coming to the door. The sunlight shone on his tanned face, and he looked strong and athletic.

"Nobody is scared," explained Bette. "We saw a light in your house last night about nine o'clock, so we were pretty sure you were back. But it seemed so quiet around the house when we came over this morning, we feared you weren't home."

"Mother wouldn't let us bother you last night," added Roy. "So here we are to check up on you this morning."

"It's good to be welcomed home by my three friends. At least I have six sharp eyes checking on my movements," said the captain with mock seriousness.

"Dad says we're pretty good at digging up facts," said Roy. "Maybe we could be detectives someday."

"He should be proud of his three live wires. I'd be glad to claim any of you as mine." Captain Timothy Lane walked over to his workbench and pulled out some boxes stacked under it, saying: "You'd better sit down, too. I want to get the weight off this leg."

"What did the doctors say about you?" asked Bette, who always said she was going to be a nurse.

"I'm doing all right, and in a few more months I'll be as good as new. Then I'll play baseball with you boys."

"That's great," declared Roy. "You've had that leg injury a long time—ever since you came home from Europe."

"Yes, it has been a long time," agreed the captain, "but I guess we can get used to almost anything, even trouble. Now tell me about yourselves. What has happened in the weeks I've been away? What have you three been doing that's exciting?"

"Getting back into the grind of school seems like a mighty big change from our vacation in the mountains where we had hiking, swimming, and boating," said Roy.

"Nothing much," said Roy with a woebegone expression. "How could we—now that school has started?"

The captain threw back his head and laughed heartily. "Don't take it so hard, Roy. You know you like school."

"I suppose we do, but it seems like a mighty big change from our vacation in the mountains where we had hiking, swimming, and motorboating."

"Wish I could have been along, Roy," said the man.

"We're looking forward to more of your stories, at least, Captain Tim. I guess they will build up our morale." Bette smiled and her eyes twinkled. "Did you know Roy and I are in the sixth grade this year?"

"It seems to me both of you should be in the same grade, shouldn't you, since you are twins?" The captain looked at Roy and Bette as he spoke. Then turning to the older brother he added: "Dick, you're in the eighth grade this year?"

"Yes, sir, and I'm studying hard. By the way, we have some questions to ask you, Captain Tim. They seem to come thick and fast when we attend classes."

"What do you know about the Bible?" asked Roy of his friend.

"The Bible!" said the captain with surprise. "What makes you think I know anything about the Bible?"

"You traveled over most of the world in both world wars," said Bette. "Surely you know about the ancient countries where the Bible was written. You see Roy and I have to write some themes about the Bible and the men and women in it."

"I could use some help in history, too," Dick pleaded.

"Wait a minute, all three of you!" implored the man, holding up his hands. "One thing at a time. What is it you want to know about the Bible?"

"Then you will help us?" asked the twins.

"Perhaps I can add a little to your knowledge," said the captain modestly. "Where I went to college we studied the Bible. That was before I was in the army."

"You were in Palestine and also in Egypt during the war, Captain Tim?"

"Yes, I was all over that region, especially during the first World War. Military duties took me from Africa to India and back to Europe."

"It must be fun to travel around the world," mused Bette.

"It's like this," explained Roy; "we never have known much

about the Bible. We have heard a few stories about such men as
Jonah, David, and Peter."

"We know the golden rule and the Beatitudes," said Bette.

"But our teacher says the Bible is the greatest book ever written, and we don't know who wrote it or when it was written."

The captain had taken a soft pine stick from the workbench
and was whittling on it with his knife. "I can tell you some of
the interesting facts about the Bible; but if I take time for your
questions, will you help me rake the leaves off the front lawn?
The autumn winds have been shaking them down while I was
away. Mrs. Lane is coming home tonight, and I want her to see
the house and yard as spick and span as I can make it."

"Won't you be glad to see her!" exclaimed Bette.

"Indeed, I will! She left for a visit in Colorado the week before I went to the hospital for treatment."

"I'll bring some asters over for a bouquet," said the girl.

"That's thoughtful, Bette. I'm sure I need your help to get the
house looking its best."

"And as for raking the lawn, of course we'll help, captain,"
said Dick.

"It's a bargain then. Now, where shall I begin about the
Bible?" mused the captain. "It is sometimes called a history, for
it tells how God loved man and what He planned for his happiness. It tells us how the world began and what happened when
man did not obey God's rules."

"How can we know more about God?" asked Dick. "It seems
hard to understand much about Him."

"I know something of how you feel, Dick, for I was puzzled
the same way once. But a grand old gentleman helped me to

2

know God better. We can see God's character in all the beautiful things He has made for us—the sunsets, the rainbows, the rivers and lakes, the moonlight shining on the trees. Surely all that beauty reveals the love of God, who made it for us. Then, too, we can see His power and greatness in the stars, the oceans, the mountains, and our world whirling through space. Besides all these, we can become acquainted with Him through His letters to us."

"You mean the Bible?" asked Bette.

"That's exactly what I mean," the captain replied. "Just as you know people better through their letters, so you can know God better by reading this Book."

"How long ago was the Bible written?" questioned Bette.

"Moses wrote some of the first books of the Bible more than fourteen hundred years before Jesus Christ was born. Moses was the author of Genesis, Exodus, Leviticus, Numbers, and Deuteronomy. They are sometimes called 'the books of Moses,' and 'the book of the law.' By the way, how many books are there in the Bible?"

"I believe there are sixty-six," replied Roy. "There are thirty-nine in the Old Testament and twenty-seven in the New Testament."

"I always remember that by the words," explained Dick. "There are three letters in *Old* and nine in *Testament.* Put the numbers together and you have thirty-nine. Then take the three and nine of *New Testament,* multiply them and you have twenty-seven—the books of the New Testament."

"That's clever, Dick, and it will help anyone to keep the number straight. As to the writers of the Bible, we know that about

The ancient scribes copied the books of the Bible with pen and ink. They usually wrote on parchment which was rolled together like this ancient manuscript to form a scroll.

forty different men wrote these books. They did not all live at the same time. It was about fifteen hundred years from the time Moses lived to the days when John wrote the last book in the Bible. The authors of the Bible had many different kinds of work. Two were kings, one was a prime minister, another was a doctor, two were fishermen, and one was a tentmaker. Some were well educated, while others had no schooling. In spite of the many men writing over this long period of time, the books have one great theme—the story of God's love for men."

"What does 'Bible' mean?" asked Roy.

"Bible means 'the books.' And it is the correct name, since it really is a library in itself. It is sometimes called 'the Scriptures,' which means 'the writings.' "

"In what language was it originally written?" asked Dick.

"Most of the Old Testament was written in Hebrew, the language of the Jews. The New Testament was in Greek, the written language used in most of the known world in the time of Christ. In those days there were no books in the form as we have

BYRON DE BOLT
AFTER J. D. PENROSE

© AUTOTYPE, AFTER J. D. PENROSE, ARTIST

The dramatic moment in the life of the Venerable Bede when he translated the last chapter
of the Gospel of John into the Anglo-Saxon language. The aged scholar died shortly afterward.

them today, for when the Bible was written there were no print-ing presses."

"Did they have to copy the writings by hand?" asked Roy.

"That's right," went on the storyteller. "All the books were written by hand, for printing had not been invented. The word *manuscript* means 'written by hand.'"

"What did books look like?" queried Bette.

"Old books were often in the form of scrolls or rolls. The writing was in columns, and the reader unrolled the roll and rolled up the part he had read."

"Who did the copying?" came the question from Roy.

"Men known as 'scribes' wrote the books, and great care was taken with the Bible to make every word perfect. When each new sheet was finished, it was checked with the original from which it had been copied, and if there was a single mistake, the copy was destroyed. In that way most errors in writing were avoided, and the Scriptures came down through the ages to us."

"Think of the days and weeks and months that it would take to copy all the books of the Bible!" exclaimed Bette.

A high priest of Samaria sitting beside the ancient and precious scrolls of the five books of Moses, called the Pentateuch.

"The scribes were required to pronounce every word aloud before they wrote it down. The name of God was so sacred to the Jews that the copyist would use a special pen and ink when he wrote God's name. They did not write on paper, but on parchment made from the skins of animals. Some of the early copies of books were written on papyrus, a kind of paper made from reeds; but this

material did not wear as well as the genuine parchment."

"When did we get the Bible in English?" asked Roy, remembering that the Scriptures were first written in Hebrew and Greek.

"It came in a roundabout way to people who read English. First, it was translated into Latin, and from the Latin into English. John Wycliffe, William Tyndale, and Miles Coverdale were Englishmen who made translations into English so that the common people could read the Bible. John Wycliffe made the first English translation in the fourteenth century. Thus we can see that the Bible has been in our language for about six hundred years."

"I have heard people talk about the King James Version. What is it?" queried Bette.

"It is the best-known version of our Bible. James I, King of England, commissioned a group of wise and devoted men to

John Wycliffe translated the Bible into the language of the common people of England
He sent many of his students forth to preach the gospel from the Book of books.

Because of persecution, William Tyndale did not dare to translate the Bible in England. But he did his work in Europe and sent the printed copies back to his homeland.

make a careful translation of the Bible for the nation. When it was published in 1611 it was known as the Authorized, or King James, Version. Its language is beautiful and noble. There are other modern versions that have been prepared by scholars; but none is loved or quoted as much as the King James Version."

"Have you read the Bible through, Captain Tim?" asked Dick.

"Yes, several times, my boy," came the answer. "And every time I read it I find many new things. There is excitement in the

When brave aviators and sailors were lost on rafts at sea during the war, the pocket edition of the Bible which they carried was a source of comfort and help to them.

Bible—stories of wars, thrilling adventures with wild animals, tales of shipwrecks, and sagas of kings and warriors who won fame and fortune."

"David killed a lion with his bare hands, I remember."

"He killed a giant, too."

"You are both right," said Captain Tim to the twins. "Without any weapon he killed both a lion and a bear. He used only his hands and arms to fight these wild beasts."

"He must have been strong," said Dick, clenching his fists as he thought of meeting a lion.

"The Bible has influenced our lives a great deal. Many famous paintings have been made to represent Bible heroes and Bible stories. Some of the greatest poetry and music have been composed about Bible themes."

"I know it is a book that helps us in time of trouble," said Bette. "I've read how it gave courage to men who were lost on rafts at sea during the war."

"One of those men was Captain Rickenbacker," said Dick. "He read the Bible to the men when they were about to give up. They prayed, and I believe their prayers were answered, for they were rescued."

"I know the Bible has been a help to me when I was in danger. I repeated the Shepherd Psalm many times when I was near the front line of battle. The wounded men loved to hear, 'The Lord is my shepherd.'" As he finished the words the captain seemed lost in memories.

"I think we'd better go," said Roy, breaking the silence. "We've kept you from your work, and we have some errands to do this morning for mother and dad. We'll see you after dinner to help rake the lawn. You've helped us a great deal in our essays for school."

"Sometime we'll have to talk about the history of the Bible lands and the people who lived there. You'll find plenty of adventure in the Bible if you look for it," said Captain Lane.

"You've made me want to read the Bible," declared Dick. "Thanks for all the time you've given us this morning, captain."

The three young people left the basement and raced across the lawn toward their home. Before they entered the front door of the Barrett house they waved at the captain, who stood watching them at the garden gate.

WHO TOLD the BATS and the SQUIRRELS?

DICK BARRETT was pedaling down Maple Street when Captain Lane called to him from the corner filling station. The boy circled back on his bicycle and rode into the driveway, where he dismounted near his friend.

"I hope I didn't stop you from an important errand," said the captain.

"Not at all, sir," young Barrett replied. "I was just heading for home. School was out a few minutes early today."

"Good enough, Dick. What I have to suggest isn't particularly important; but I wondered if you would like to go with me to the farm."

"Would I?" answered Dick eagerly. "Nothing would suit me better, Captain Tim. During school this afternoon I kept wishing I could be out of doors. Do you ever feel crowded by houses and buildings?"

"Yes, I know how you feel. Sometimes I want to get away from work and study. After all, there's nothing like the fresh air and open country to make you breathe deeper."

"And you don't feel tied down, either," added the boy.

"That's it," agreed the man. "By the way, do you suppose the twins would enjoy going with us? There's plenty of room in the car."

"Of course they would," exclaimed young Barrett. "Suppose I ride on home, captain, and put my bicycle away? Then I'll see if it is all right with mother for us to go."

"That's a good idea, and I'll be along in a few minutes. I think Joe is about through greasing the car."

Twenty minutes later Dick and the twins, Bette and Roy, were in the car with Captain Lane, driving east on the highway toward the farms and orchards nestled among the rolling hills.

"I haven't been out to the farm since I returned from my trip," explained the man. He took his foot off the throttle as the car approached a railroad crossing. "Mrs. Lane wants some apples and pumpkins, and anything else that looks good to eat."

"There's no end to good things on Hillcrest Farm," Bette declared, her eyes sparkling. "I remember when we were there in June the strawberries and cherries were ripe."

"Mother Barlow had made a batch of cookies and doughnuts, too. I felt as if I wanted to stay there always," added Roy.

"I guess that's one of the joys of the farm I miss most," mused Captain Lane. "Of course, Mr. and Mrs. Barlow manage it for me and we get lots of good things to eat, and some profits, too. But it isn't the same as living there."

"You grew up on Hillcrest Farm, didn't you, Captain Tim?" asked Roy.

"Yes, the farm belonged to my father. I was a farmer until I was called into the army during the first World War. That seems like a long time ago."

"The Barlows took charge of the place for you when you went away?"

"That's right, Bette, and they have lived there ever since. They love Hillcrest Farm almost as much as I do," the captain admitted.

"Aren't you going to get Chips while you are out here?" questioned Roy.

"Yes, indeed," was the reply. "In fact, that is one of the principal reasons I'm driving out today. We certainly miss the dog around the house." Chips was Captain and Mrs. Lane's brown cocker spaniel who had been left with the Barlows while his owners were away.

"We're almost to Hillcrest Farm now," said Bette.

"It's around the next bend," agreed the captain. "I remember when going to Middletown and back took almost half a day. Now we drive it in less than a half hour."

"Perhaps you'll be flying in your own plane one of these days," suggested Dick, who was interested in aviation. "Lots of farmers are getting airplanes."

"I'm probably too old-fashioned, Dick," said the man with a laugh. "I still prefer four wheels on the ground."

The captain stopped the car at the white gate, and Dick jumped out to open it. As he drew back the bolt, a dog came bounding down the driveway. "Look, Captain Tim, here comes Chips," shouted Roy. "Is he glad to see you!"

The man opened the door of the car and a ball of fur bounced into his lap, whining and licking his master's hands in welcome. "Well, Chips, are you glad to see me? Did you think I was never coming to get you?" asked the captain, patting the silky head.

Roy and Bette picked apples while Dick gathered a basket of pecans. Captain Lane brought in a box of Concord grapes.

Bette and Roy could sit still no longer. They jumped from the car and ran ahead to the large two-story house where a white-haired woman was standing on the back porch. "Hello, Mother Barlow," they said in unison as they hurried up the steps.

"If it isn't the Barrett twins," said Mrs. Barlow putting an arm around each of the children, as they sat down on the porch lounge beside her. "You came with the captain, I suppose."

"Yes, we did. Here he comes now. Chips wouldn't let his master drive on until he had been properly welcomed," Roy explained.

As the car stopped, the captain spoke: "You seem to be waiting for us with your same cheery smile, Mother Barlow."

"It's good to see you home again," said the woman.

"Home never looked better to me, and Hillcrest Farm seems almost like home, too." Captain Lane looked toward the red barn standing on the hill. Beyond was the orchard and meadow where the horses grazed. "How is the apple crop by this time?"

"It's very good, so my husband says. He's out in the orchard picking some Winesaps right now." The woman untied her apron as she spoke. "Would you like to have me find him for you?" she asked.

"No, never mind, Mother Barlow. We'll walk out that way," said the captain, picking up a bucket near the steps. "I want some apples and pumpkins."

"You'll want some grapes, too. They're at their best. And the pecans are beginning to drop," the woman explained. "I'll put a jar of cream and a basket of eggs in the car for Mrs. Lane."

"You think of everything. I know my wife will be asking for the cream before I'm in the house," Captain Lane declared.

Mrs. Barlow came out of the house to welcome her visitors. She put her arms around the twins as she said in a cheery voice: "You came with the captain, I suppose."

While he was chatting, the three Barretts started for the orchard with Chips at their heels. "I guess it's time for me to follow my runaways, so excuse me, Mother Barlow," called the man as he started across the farmyard.

After meeting Farmer Barlow, Roy and Bette volunteered to pick apples while the captain talked with his farm manager. Soon the twins were climbing ladders and chattering merrily as they pulled the red and golden balls from the trees.

"I'll take a bucket and gather pecans from under the trees down by the creek," suggested Dick, who knew the farm well.

"A great idea," agreed Captain Lane. "We'll meet you there in about fifteen minutes."

Dick Barrett had filled his bucket with choice nuts and was sitting in the shade when the men arrived with boxes of grapes.

Bette and Roy also came into view carrying buckets of apples.

"Let's sit here and rest a few minutes after our work," suggested the captain. "You look comfortable, Dick."

"I'm enjoying it, Captain Tim," the boy exclaimed. "I've been watching the squirrels gather nuts. You should see those bushy-tailed fellows work. I've never seen them busier than they are today."

"They're hard workers, all right," Farmer Barlow agreed. "Have you ever noticed that they never bury all their nuts in one hole? Instead, they hide them in different places. That's good sense, too, for if someone finds their nuts in one hole, they always have another storehouse to depend on."

"Look at those two young squirrels!" As he spoke, Captain Lane pointed toward a limb where the animals were scampering. "They were born this spring. They have never seen snow or winter weather. How do they know that there won't be nuts on the trees all the year round? Something tells them to hide the nuts so that they will have food during the cold, bleak months."

"That's called 'instinct,' " the farmer declared.

"Yes, but what is instinct, Barlow? Who gave the animals that clever bit of knowledge?" returned the captain.

"Hum! That's another question I can't answer," admitted the farm manager.

"God must have told the squirrels how to plan for winter," said Bette thoughtfully.

"I'm sure you're right," Captain Lane nodded in approval. "When we study the animals we find that the Creator who made them was wise. The squirrel isn't the only creature that plans ahead for his food. The ant does the same thing, and Solomon once said: 'Go to the ant, thou sluggard; consider her ways, and be wise.'"

"We saw the seals on the rocks near Golden Gate at San Francisco," Dick began. "We were told that some of them swim for thousands of miles across the ocean; but they come back again each year to the same rocks. How do they know the way? They do not have a compass to guide them as does the captain of a ship. They haven't maps or charts to help them find their way."

"That's right, Dick, a wise Creator must have given the animals wonderful instincts to help them," said the captain.

"While you're talking about smart animals and sea creatures," put in Farmer Barlow, "I'll have to tell you about Sandy. He was a dog we owned years ago in Tennessee. We raised him from a puppy, and he went everywhere with my father. Once we moved to another farm some five hundred miles away, and we left Sandy with my uncle until we could get settled. Then we were going to send for him. Well, we got a letter from my uncle saying Sandy had run away. It made us all wish we had brought the dog with us. But about a month later, who should come trotting into

w do the young squirrels know that they should re up nuts for the winter? They have never seen e snow fall or searched for food in the winter.

3

the barnyard one day but Sandy! He looked tired and he ate like a wolf for days after he arrived. He had found our trail some way and had followed us five hundred miles to our new home. You may be sure he was happy to see us."

"I read of a dog that made his way across the United States from California back to his home in Kentucky," Bette declared.

"Do you know how bats fly in the dark without crashing into things?" asked Captain Lane.

"No," said Roy with a smile. "Do they fly blind like aviators?"

"Well, at least they have a radar system to help them," replied the man.

"Wait a minute!" exclaimed Dick with sudden interest. "You mean bats have a radar system like that used by ships and airplanes?"

"That's right," the captain continued. "Scientists wondered for years how bats could fly in complete darkness without having accidents. They blindfolded some bats, but the creatures could fly in a room where wires had been strung between the walls just as well as they could when they could see. Finally, the men found that the bats were helpless if their ears were stopped up or their mouths were taped shut."

"This sounds mysterious. What did their ears and mouths have to do with seeing how to fly?" questioned Bette.

"The scientists obtained some special instruments which record sounds man cannot hear. These machines were placed in the room with the bats, and it was discovered that a bat made high-pitched cries when he flew in the dark. As the echo of his sounds came back to his ears, he knew he was near some object, and his brain told him to dodge it."

"That certainly is like radar," Roy spoke up quickly. "An airplane using radar sends out radio waves, and the echo comes back to the receiver if there is an object in the way of the waves."

"Think of bats having that system long before man discovered it," said Dick with amazement in his eyes.

"I can understand the Bible story better, Captain Tim, where it says God saw everything He had made and it was good." Bette looked at the squirrels as she spoke. "If we knew all the wonders of animal life," she added, "we would trust God more."

"I'm getting chilly in the shade," said Farmer Barlow. "If I don't get to moving I'll have some sore joints tomorrow."

"If we don't get to moving," returned the captain, "we won't be home before dark, since the sun is setting early these autumn days. Shall we start for the house with our buckets and boxes?"

Radar instruments send radio waves out into the air and the echoes come back to the delicate receiver if there is an object standing in the path of the electronic waves.

ACME NEWSPICTURES, INC.

"Let's go!" agreed Dick.

"The time went too fast," Bette moaned. "I hoped to have a ride on Peggy." The girl was thinking of the favorite saddle horse of Hillcrest Farm.

"That will have to wait until next time, I'm afraid," said the captain. "We'll plan a day of it then."

Within a few minutes the car was loaded with fruit, nuts, and pumpkins, and Captain Lane started the car down the driveway with three Barretts waving and Chips barking good-by to Mr. and Mrs. Barlow.

"What fun we've had at Hillcrest Farm this afternoon," Dick said as he munched a juicy apple.

"It would be fun to live on a farm," mused Bette, thinking of the horseback ride she had missed. "I could have a saddle horse of my own, then."

The car gathered speed as it turned onto the highway and headed west. The last rays of the sun spread across the sky.

"Look at that V formation of geese flying south," said the captain. "We know that cold weather isn't far off." Three pairs of eyes followed the man's finger as he pointed ahead to where a flock of geese was winging its way through the chilly evening air.

"They are in perfect formation," Dick commented, comparing them to a group of airplanes.

"Since you are interested in aviation, Dick, tell us why geese fly that way," suggested the captain.

"I'd never thought much about it," the boy replied. "I suppose one of the main reasons is to protect them from their enemies. That is why planes fly that way in battle."

"It's a good reason. Then, too, the leader keeps the flock to-

The geese fly in a V formation like war planes to protect them from enemies and also to make it easier to follow the course that the leader chooses for the flock.

gether better, and this makes flying easier for the big birds."

"The leaders change places sometimes, don't they?" queried Dick.

"Yes, when the leader becomes tired, he falls back and another bird in the flock takes his place. They fly swiftly, too. Did you know that, during the war, radar operators followed flocks of geese with their instruments and found that they flew at an average speed of thirty-five miles an hour?"

"Those geese are flying as if they knew the way perfectly, Captain Tim," Bette spoke as she watched the birds fading into small specks against the clouds. "They remind me of the poem we learned in school last week by William Cullen Bryant. After he had seen a waterfowl flying in the sky one evening he wrote:

> " 'Whither, midst falling dew,
> While glow the heavens with the last steps of day,
> Far, through their rosy depths, dost thou pursue
> Thy solitary way?' "

"This is an ideal setting for that poem, Bette," said the captain. "Didn't the poet say something about God's care for the bird?"

"Yes, I imagine you are thinking of the lines that go like this:

> " 'There is a Power whose care
> Teaches thy way along that pathless coast—
> The desert and illimitable air—
> Lone wandering, but not lost.'

"And in the last stanza the poet says:

> " 'He who, from zone to zone,
> Guides through the boundless sky thy certain flight,
> In the long way that I must tread alone,
> Will lead my steps aright.' "

"I guess Bryant knew what he was talking about, all right," mused the man at the wheel.

"Look at the golden sunset," exclaimed Bette. "Isn't the great out-of-doors beautiful!"

"Remember the sunsets on our vacation trip?" suggested Roy. "There were snow-capped mountains and blue lakes surrounded by pine and fir trees. It was something one will never forget."

"It is a wonderful world—and a big one, too," Captain Lane affirmed.

"It looks big from an airplane," Dick added. "Dad gave me a trip with him on my birthday last summer. When you look down on the mountains and valleys, the rivers and farms, you wonder how it was made."

"Our earth and all the plant and animal life didn't just happen," said the captain. "There was a great Designer who planned the world and made it. For example, if you were given a watch, Dick, you might take it apart and put the pieces in a box. But how long do you suppose you would have to shake the box before all the wheels and springs would fit together into a perfect watch?"

"It could never put itself together again, Captain Tim," said Dick.

"Neither could our world, whirling through space with more than two billion human beings on it, have had its beginning without a Creator. Therefore, when we think about the earth and all the animals and people on it, we ask: How did it start? Well, one can find the true story of its origin in the Bible."

"I'll begin reading my Bible tonight, captain," said Dick Barrett. "Where will I find the story of how our world was made?"

"Yes, tell us," urged Bette. "I want to read it, too."

"Just begin at the first chapter of Genesis, the first book of the Bible. You will find that the story of creation is a wonderful prose poem."

"Will that also tell us about the first man and the first woman?" asked Roy.

"Yes, the fascinating story of Adam and Eve is there, too. If you start reading, you'll meet them, as well as their sons, Cain and Abel."

Father and Mother Barrett sat on the sofa, Dick stretched out in front of the fireplace, and Bette sat in her favorite chair, while Roy began reading from the Bible.

As the auto stopped at the curb in front of the Barrett home, three happy adventurers thanked their host for the good time and trooped up the walk and into the house, their arms loaded with boxes and bags of fruit and nuts.

Later that evening after dinner, when Mother Barrett and Bette had washed the dishes and completed their work in the kitchen, Roy got his Bible and turned to the book of Genesis.

"I was planning to read my Bible, too," Bette declared as she entered the living room and sat down in her favorite chair.

"So was I," spoke up Dick.

"Let's read the first chapter of Genesis together," suggested the girl. "Roy can read it to all of us."

Father Barrett put down his newspaper and Mother Barrett sat on the sofa beside him. Dick stretched himself full length on the rug in front of the glowing logs in the fireplace, while his brother pulled his chair closer to the floor lamp and began to read.

This is the story of creation as Roy read it from the Bible:

"In the beginning God created the heaven and the earth. And the earth was without form, and void; and darkness was upon the face of the deep. And the Spirit of God moved upon the face of the waters. And God said, Let there be light: and there was light. And God saw the light, that it was good: and God divided the light from the darkness. And God called the light Day, and the darkness He called Night. And the evening and the morning were the first day.

"And God said, Let there be a firmament in the midst of the waters, and let it divide the waters from the waters. And God made the firmament, and divided the waters which were under the firmament from the waters which were above the firmament: and it was so. And God called the firmament Heaven. And the evening and the morning were the second day. And God said, Let the waters under the heaven be gathered together unto one place, and let the dry land appear: and it was so. And God called the dry land Earth; and the gathering together of the waters called He Seas: and God saw that it was good. And God said, Let the earth bring forth grass, the herb yielding seed, and the fruit tree yielding fruit after his kind, whose seed is in itself, upon the earth: and it was so. And the earth brought forth grass, and herb yielding seed after his kind, and the tree yielding fruit, whose seed was in itself, after his kind: and God saw that it was good. And the evening and the morning were the third day.

"And God said, Let there be lights in the firmament of the

heaven to divide the day from the night; and let them be for signs, and for seasons, and for days, and years: and let them be for lights in the firmament of the heaven to give light upon the earth: and it was so. And God made two great lights; the greater light to rule the day, and the lesser light to rule the night: He made the stars also. And God set them in the firmament of the heaven to give light upon the earth, and to rule over the day and over the night, and to divide the light from the darkness: and God saw that it was good. And the evening and the morning were the fourth day. And God said, Let the waters bring forth abundantly the moving creature that hath life, and fowl that may fly above the earth in the open firmament of heaven. And God created great whales, and every living creature that moveth, which the waters brought forth abundantly, after their kind, and every winged fowl after his kind: and God saw that it was good. And God blessed them, saying, Be fruitful, and multiply, and fill the waters in the seas, and let fowl multiply in the earth. And the evening and the morning were the fifth day.

"And God said, Let the earth bring forth the living creature after his kind, cattle, and creeping thing, and beast of the earth after his kind: and it was so. And God made the beast of the earth after his kind, and cattle after their kind, and everything that creepeth upon the earth after his kind: and God saw that it was good. And God said, Let Us make man in Our image, after Our likeness: and let them have dominion over the fish of the sea, and over the fowl of the air, and over the cattle, and over all the earth, and over every creeping thing that creepeth upon the earth. So God created man in His own image, in the image of God created He him; male and female created He them. And

God blessed them, and God said unto them, Be fruitful, and multiply, and replenish the earth, and subdue it: and have dominion over the fish of the sea, and over the fowl of the air, and over every living thing that moveth upon the earth.

"And God said, Behold, I have given you every herb bearing seed, which is upon the face of all the earth, and every tree, in the which is the fruit of a tree yielding seed; to you it shall be for meat. And to every beast of the earth, and to every fowl of the air, and to everything that creepeth upon the earth, wherein there is life, I have given every green herb for meat: and it was so. And God saw everything that He had made, and, behold, it was very good. And the evening and the morning were the sixth day.

"Thus the heavens and the earth were finished, and all the host of them. And on the seventh day God ended His work which He had made; and He rested on the seventh day from all His work which He had made. And God blessed the seventh day, and sanctified it: because that in it He had rested from all His work which God created and made." Genesis 1:1-31; 2:1-3.

There are many marvelous secrets and wonders to be discovered in nature if the boy or girl will spend time studying and enjoying God's great out-of-doors.

1

A WORLD Is Made

GENESIS 1; 2

WE LOVE to go back to the beginning of things. How did they start? We see a sturdy, wide-spreading oak in the meadow. It has endured the storms and winds for almost a hundred years. But how did it begin? You pick up a tiny acorn and find that it holds the secret of the oak tree. A brown acorn, cold and hard almost like a rock, falls into the ground. The sunshine and rain do their work, and soon the life hidden within that shell sends forth shoots that eventually grow into a strong tree.

We see a caterpillar clinging to a leaf on a garden bush. Day after day we see it as we pass by. It changes to a lifeless-looking cocoon; but one warm morning we discover life stirring in this crinkly lump, and soon a gorgeous butterfly emerges and dries its silky wings.

Life is a strange mystery. Where and how is the life hidden in the acorn? How does the caterpillar produce a perfect specimen of a butterfly? How can life come from the robin's eggs in the nest hidden among the thick branches? Where did life come from in the first place?

Let us go back to the time when there was no life on this earth. We shall start at the beginning of our world. "When God

(43)

began to create the heavens and the earth, the earth was a desolate waste, with darkness covering the abyss and a tempestuous wind raging over the surface of the waters." Yes, our earth was a dreary, shapeless mass, and there were no plants or animals, and there was no dry land. What a strange, dismal picture—no life, no moving creatures, no sound, no light!

Then the all-wise, loving God began to make the world into a beautiful home in which men and animals could live. As He thought of the world in darkness He commanded: "Let there be light!" When He spoke, rays of light broke through the blackness; more and more light shone upon the shapeless, water-covered earth. This was the first morning of the world's history. But if we could have looked at the dismal scene we would not

One warm spring morning we may discover life stirring in the caterpillar, and soon a gorgeous butterfly emerges from the crinkly lump and dries its silky wings.

W. WILKE, ARTIST

On the first day of creation week God said: "Let there be light!" Rays of light broke through the dense blackness and shone down upon the shapeless water-covered earth.

have thought it an attractive place for a home. God saw the light and called it Day, and the darkness He called Night.

On the second day God spoke again, and the water on the earth was separated from the water above the earth. The clear blue dome of the sky appeared, and God called it Heaven. We know that the sky is filled with air which extends above the earth's surface for miles, and that the water in the atmosphere is carried by clouds that float in the air. As the second day of creation closed, the earth had fresh air and light. Since both of these are necessary in order for plants and animals to live, we can see how God was preparing a home for man.

On the third day God said: "Let the waters below the sky be

On the second day God spoke again, and the water on the earth was separated from the water above the earth. The clear dome of heaven appeared for the first time.

gathered into one place so that the dry land may appear!" Then the waters on the earth rolled and tumbled together to become oceans, and dry land arose above the seas for the first time. The mountains stood out tall and majestic, and the valleys and plains were spread over the earth; but the hills and plains were not beautiful, for they were barren.

Sometimes we have seen the scarred, bare earth after a river has overflowed its banks. The new world without grass or trees must have looked like land that has been flooded. Therefore God continued His work and said: "Let the earth produce vegetation, seed-bearing plants, and the various kinds of fruit trees that bear fruit containing their seed!" And it was so, for the trees, grasses, and plants sprang from the fresh black soil that only the day before had been covered with water. The seeds of plants and grasses can be depended upon to obey the laws of nature, which are God's rules. If we plant beans, they will produce beanstalks. If we plant corn, then we can expect corn to grow. The seeds produce plants after their kind. As God looked upon the world carpeted with green grass and adorned with flowers of every color, as He saw the beautiful trees loaded with many kinds of fruit, He said that it was all good.

Trees, grass, and flowers grow best in the sunlight. Therefore on the fourth day God caused the sun to appear. Its warm rays shone on the mountains and glistened on the rivers flowing through the valleys. In the evening, after the sun had set, behold, the moon and stars appeared. God commanded the sun and moon to give light, and also to separate day from night. He

The waters rolled together and there was dry land on the third day when God said: "Let the waters below the sky be gathered into one place so that the dry land may appear!"

said: "Let them serve for signs, for fixed times, and for days and years." The millions of stars that astronomers have seen and photographed with the aid of telescopes are really great suns, as large or larger than our sun. Each one was made by the all-powerful Creator. The sun is really a blazing star that is near enough to our earth to give it light and heat. Its atomic energy makes it possible for plants, animals, and man to live and grow. We set our clocks by the position of the stars in the heavens. We mark the length of the year by the time it takes for our earth to make a complete trip around the sun. We divide the year into months according to the movement of the moon. Truly, the sun, moon, and stars are the clock of the heavens to mark off years, seasons, and months. They obey the rules of their Creator, and they can be depended upon for their exactness of motion.

On the fifth day God created the fish that live in the seas and rivers; He also made the birds and insects that fly in the air. The new world suddenly came to life with the flash of wings. The fish jumped in the rivers, while bees buzzed and crickets chirped among the flowers and grass. Great whales glided through the sea and spouted when they came to the surface for air. Bluebirds, orioles, parrots, eagles, ducks, pigeons, ostriches; yes, birds of every color and size were to be seen. Birds with bright-colored plumage perched in the trees, while songbirds made the air ring with sweet melodies—earth's first music. Once more, at the close of the fifth day, God looked upon His work and saw that it was good.

On the sixth day God made the land animals and reptiles. Think of the many creatures that roamed the earth that day for the first time! The forests and fields were suddenly alive with

The sun appeared on the fourth day of creation, and that night the moon and stars gave light. God said: "Let them serve for signs, for fixed times, and for days and years."

elephants, lions, horses, cows, monkeys, kangaroos, giraffes, and a thousand other animals! Many of the creatures that lived then were much larger than the ones we see in zoos today. The bones of giant animals have been found buried in the earth, and you may see some of them in museums. The earth, covered with green grass and made glorious with trees and flowers, was now filled with the melodies of birds and the sounds of the animals. The deer leaped through the grass. The bears climbed up into the trees; the lions roved about the forest. But the animals were not wild or savage as they are today. Above was the blue sky and warm sunlight—signs of God's love. But still something was lacking. There were no people to enjoy this perfect home.

The fish that swim in the seas and rivers and the birds and insects that fly in the air were made on the fifth day of creation week. And God saw that His work was good.

God said: "Let Us make man in Our image." From the dust of the earth He formed a body the shape of a man. It was made in the likeness of God Himself. Then the Creator breathed into the clay body the breath of life, and, behold, a living human being! There was the perfect head with eyes to see, ears to hear,

On the sixth day God made the many kinds of land animals and reptiles. Then, as His crowning work He created man from the dust, saying: "Let Us make man in Our image."

and a mouth to speak. There were strong arms to move swiftly and sturdy legs to carry the man wherever he wanted to go. This was truly a wonderful being, made in the Creator's own image.

We know today that the elements in the soil are the same as those that we have in our bodies, but only the mighty God could take the dust of the earth, form man from it, and give him life. Man was strong and healthy. He could think and speak; he could run; he could swim in the river; he could work. He loved his Creator, and listened to all of His instructions. His eyes were keen; his ears could hear the song of the birds and the rustle of the leaves.

Adam, the first man, walked through the forests. He saw the lions and the tigers, the squirrels, the birds in the trees, and the eagle soaring high in the air. When Adam grew hungry, what should he eat? He remembered that God had said: "I give you all the seed-bearing plants that are found all over the earth, and all the trees which have seed-bearing fruit; it shall be yours to eat." Perhaps the man saw some luscious red strawberries and decided to pick one and put it in his mouth. How good it tasted! He picked an orange and sampled its delicious flavor. Or, as he walked under the trees he found walnuts or pecans, which he shelled and ate. The beautiful new world had food in abundance for man.

Some of the animals followed Adam, and he watched each one. He saw the elephant swing his trunk and look at him with sharp little eyes. The deer was curious and came close to the man. God had all the animals pass before Adam, and he gave names to every one. Would you like to have named the birds and animals? Adam had to think of many names to fit the creatures. He saw that all of them had mates. But among them there was not one found who was like man. He began to feel lonely. Was there no one on the earth who could be his companion?

While Adam was considering his plight, God caused him to

fall into a deep sleep, and He opened man's side and took out one of his ribs. God formed the rib into another beautiful creature— a woman. Here is a wonderful lesson. The woman who becomes the wife of a man is to stand beside him as his equal. She is not above him—not below him. She is to love her husband and to be his companion in life.

God brought the woman to the man, and he loved her and she became his wife. And Adam gave her the name Eve because she was the mother of all living beings.

At the close of the sixth day God looked upon the earth filled with living creatures, who were to be ruled by the man and woman, and He saw that everything He had made was very good.

The task of creating the world was finished in only six days! God's crowning work was man, who was formed in the image of his Creator. Adam and Eve were given dominion over the earth and all the animals in it.

On the seventh day God rested from His work. He made the seventh day of the week a special occasion in honor of the new world which He had created. God blessed the seventh day and set it apart from the other six days of the week as a time for man to rest and to remember the One who made the world and created man. We should remember the Sabbath, for it is the special day of the week when we are to go to church to worship and honor our Creator, and thank Him for our beautiful world. We should love to go to church and listen to God's word on the Sabbath, and we enjoy going out in nature to study His wonderful works.

2

An ENEMY in the GARDEN

GENESIS 3

DID Adam and Eve have the whole world for their home? Where did they live? Did Adam build a house for them to live in? These are questions we naturally ask when we read of the new world and of the first man and woman.

When the Creator made the earth, He planned an ideal home for Adam and Eve. It was the Garden of Eden. A river flowed through this park and watered the trees and plants. Adam and his wife were to care for the trees, the plants, and the vines, and to watch over the animals.

The happy couple did not have a house such as we live in today, for the weather was perfect—it was neither cold nor hot, neither was there rain, for a mist "used to rise from the earth and water all the surface of the ground." There was a beautiful bower for Adam and Eve to sleep in. Its walls were climbing vines entwined with fragrant flowers. Birds warbled softly in the branches above them, and soft grass made a living carpet for their feet.

Think of suddenly living in a perfect world and discovering the wonders of nature. Adam and Eve could walk about in their Eden home and watch the strutting peacock on the grass; they

(55)

The Garden of Eden, the most beautiful spot on the newly created earth, was given to Adam and Eve to keep as their home.

must have laughed as they saw the monkeys swinging in the trees, or saw the elephant spraying water over himself with his trunk. The squirrels jumped from limb to limb in the treetops, and lions, as gentle as lambs, followed them. They must have watched the bees gathering honey and observed the mother kangaroo carrying her baby in her pouch. They stood on the bank of the river where white swans glided by and quacking ducks fed on the lush grass. Adam gathered fruit and nuts from the trees and brought them to his wife. They sat in the shade and enjoyed the delicacies together.

On the seventh day of each week they rested from their work and worshiped God. The Creator talked with Adam and Eve, explaining the wonders of the world to them and telling them how they could continue to be perfectly happy.

But like many persons today, Adam and Eve looked with longing at something that was not theirs. Eden had many trees loaded with fruit, and the man and woman had all that they could eat. Now, there were two trees about which Adam and Eve were given special instructions. One tree, called "the tree of life," had rich, life-giving fruit.

There was another special tree in the garden called "the tree of the knowledge of good and evil." Wonderful fruit grew on this tree; but Adam and Eve were told not to eat of it. The Lord God said to Adam: "From every tree in the garden you are free to eat; but from the tree of the knowledge of good and evil you must not eat; for the day that you eat of it you shall certainly die." God asked the man and woman to trust Him and to obey His words. Surely they loved their Creator enough to keep His rules, for in obeying them they would find true happiness. If they wanted their own selfish way they could do as they pleased, but it would bring them sorrow and pain. Would you have obeyed God if you had lived in that garden home?

One day when Eve was walking alone in the park, the serpent—a wise and clever creature—spoke to her from the branches of the tree of the knowledge of good and evil. The woman was surprised and startled to hear this strange, musical voice, so she stopped and looked at the beautiful serpent. It was eating some of the rich-looking fruit of the forbidden tree. Now Satan, the evil one, who is sometimes called the devil, was talking through the serpent. He asked Eve: "So God has said that you are not to eat from any tree of the garden?"

Eve quickly answered: "From the fruit of the trees of the garden we may eat; it is only concerning the fruit of the tree which is in the middle of the garden that God has said, 'You may not eat any of it, nor touch it, lest you die.'"

"You would not die at all," said the serpent to the woman, "for God knows that the very day you eat of it, your eyes will be opened, and you will be like gods who know good from evil."

The woman listened to these lying words. She forgot the warning of God, and she looked at the fruit of the tree of the knowledge of good and evil. It seemed to be good to eat. She wondered if God really meant what He said. Eve could not take her eyes from the tree. If she could only taste the fruit! She started to pick some of it, but then she drew back. She remembered God's words concerning the fruit of this tree: "You may not eat any of it." Then suddenly the serpent picked the fruit and offered it to Eve. "You will be like gods who know good from evil," echoed in her ear. She wanted to be great; she longed

N. BRICE, ARTIST

© P. P. P. A.

The woman was surprised to hear the serpent speak and she listened to his words. Finally she took the fruit from the forbidden tree of the knowledge of good and evil.

to be wise. Perhaps if she ate the fruit she would be like God. The woman snatched the fruit from the serpent and ate it.

Then Eve thought of Adam, and she picked some of the forbidden fruit and carried it to him, and he ate it. They both knew they had disobeyed God's command, and they were ashamed. The Creator had made this tree a test to man. If Adam and Eve had truly loved God they would have obeyed Him and left the fruit of this tree alone. To disobey God and break His rules is sin.

When evening came, the man and woman heard the Lord God walking in the garden. He was looking for them; but

Adam and Eve did not want to see God. They hid among the trees, hoping that He would not find them.

"Where are you?" God called to the man.

Adam could not hide when the Lord spoke to him, so he said: "I heard the sound of You in the garden, and I was afraid, . . . so I hid myself." Adam, created in the image of God, was afraid of his Creator because he had broken the rules of his new home.

The Lord said: "Have you eaten from the tree from which I commanded you not to eat?"

The man hung his head. He did not want to admit his wrong, so he tried to excuse himself by saying: "The woman whom You set at my side, it was she who gave me fruit from the tree; so I ate it."

God turned to Eve. "Whatever have you done?" He asked.

Eve did not want to admit her sin, and she answered: "It was the serpent that misled me, and so I ate it."

Because it had spoken the lie of Satan, the serpent was cursed. God said:

> "Because you have done this,
> The most cursed of all animals shall you be,
> And of all wild beasts."

Perhaps this is one reason why snakes are quite generally hated today.

Sad were the words the Lord spoke to the man and the woman. He told Eve that she would have pain and sorrow because she disobeyed. He told Adam that his work would be much harder, for now thorns, thistles, and weeds would grow on the earth. He would sweat and grow tired at his labor. Be-

cause they had broken the rules of the garden home, the man and woman could no longer enjoy it. They must leave it and go to another part of the world. They could never eat of the fruit of the tree of life again; they could not sit on the bank of the river of life. Because of their sin they would grow old, and someday they would die.

But the Creator loved Adam and Eve even though they had broken His rules. He gave them a promise that was like a light in the darkness. He said:

> "I will put enmity between you and the woman,
> And between your posterity and hers;
> They shall attack you in the head,
> And you shall attack them in the heel."

It meant that there would be conflict between Eve's children and the evil one. And someday Satan, who had deceived them, would be destroyed. A Hero would be born among men who would fight the enemy. This Hero would be Jesus, God's only Son, and He would gain the victory over Satan. Adam and Eve could look with hope to the time when Jesus would come from heaven to pay the penalty for man's sin. They did not realize He would not come in their lifetime; but the bright promise of a Redeemer would burn in the hearts of men until He came to "save His people from their sins."

Now that Adam and Eve were leaving the Garden of Eden, they needed clothing to shield them from briers and thorns that were springing up, and also to protect them from the chilling winds. God gave them coats made from the skins of animals. Wonderful is His love, for He thought of His children's needs and cared for them even though they had disobeyed Him.

An angel with a flaming sword stood guard at the entrance of Eden to keep Adam and Eve from returning to their idyllic home.
S. P. C. K., A. DIXON, ARTIST

When Adam and Eve left their garden home, they began to understand how much sin had cost; they saw the first briers and thorns, and watched the leaves fall from the trees.

It was a sad day when God led the man and woman out of the garden. No longer could they come and talk with Him as they had in their Eden home. Never again did Adam and Eve walk in that idyllic park which God had given them, for an angel with a sword of fire was sent to stand guard at the entrance. As the sun set that evening, there were tears in the eyes of the man and woman. They were beginning to understand how their own selfishness had destroyed their happiness.

3

When CAIN HATED His BROTHER

GENESIS 4

As ADAM and Eve left the gate of the Garden of Eden to seek shelter in the world, they were sad and lonely. If they had been afraid in their beautiful home after they had broken God's rules, they were much more fearful now in the strange land where they had never been before.

The man and woman needed a place to live, so Adam built a shelter. He found that he had to work harder to get food. Eve saw the first briers and thorns; she watched the first leaves fall from the trees, and these reminded her of the blight on nature that was the result of sin.

But in spite of the hardships that came to them, Adam and Eve never forgot the promise of a Saviour. Again and again they went back to the gate of the Garden of Eden to worship God. To help man remember that someday he would be saved from sin, the Lord told Adam to take a lamb from his flock and kill it. The lamb had done no wrong; but when Adam took the life of the innocent creature, he realized more vividly that sin caused death. He longed for the day when Jesus, "the Lamb of God," would come to take away the sin of the world.

Wouldn't this be a strange world if it were the home of only two persons? It was God's plan that many more people should live on the earth. So there came a day when a son was born to Eve. The happy father and mother named the baby Cain. They hoped he would be the Hero who would save mankind by overcoming Satan. As a boy, Cain helped his father plant the seeds and harvest the grain in the field. He listened to the story of the creation of the world from his father Adam.

After a time another baby came to the family. Eve named her second son Abel. When the boy grew old enough to go out into the field, he helped his father care for the sheep. Adam told Cain and Abel that God's Son would someday come to earth to save men from sin. When the boys saw their father kill a lamb and offer it as a sacrifice, they knew that it was to remind them of the coming Saviour.

When Cain grew older he decided he wanted to be a farmer. He sowed the seeds and cared for the growing plants.

Cain became a farmer, sowing the seed, plowing the ground, and reaping the harvest; while Abel chose to raise sheep on the rich pasture land not far from his father's home.

W. WILKE, ARTIST

Abel obeyed God's command and brought an offering which pleased the Lord; but Cain did as he pleased and his gift was rejected because he refused to obey the word of God.

Abel chose to be a shepherd. He cared for his sheep in the rich pasture land not far from his father's home.

A day came when Cain and Abel brought an offering to God. Each of the brothers gathered stones and piled them up to make an altar as their father had done. Cain brought a basket of fruits and grains from his field and orchard as his offering. He was strong and he had worked hard. He was proud of his harvest, but he forgot the promise of God and did not bring a lamb as an offering.

Abel loved the Lord and followed His commands. He brought a lamb, killed it, and placed it on his altar. He looked forward to the coming of the Lamb of God, the Saviour promised to Adam and Eve who would free them from sin.

Abel's offering pleased the Lord; but Cain's gift was not ac-

cepted. And because his offering did not find favor, Cain became furious. God saw him and said: "Why are you angry, and
why are you downcast? If you have been doing right, should
you not be happy? But if you have not, sin will be lurking at the
door." By these words Cain knew he had disobeyed; but he was
not sorry for his mistake. He was not only angry, but he hated
Abel because his offering was accepted.

Cain allowed this black sin of hatred to grow until it filled
his heart. One day the two men were in the field together. Cain
quarreled with his younger brother and lost his temper. In his
fury he struck Abel. The younger brother fell to the ground.

Adam and Eve were heartbroken when they found the lifeless body of their youngest
son. But their tears of grief or sorrow for sin could not bring Abel back to them.

A. BOUGUEREAU, ARTIST   © RISCHGITZ STUDIOS

Cain ran to him, but Abel did not move or cry out. He was dead! This was the terrible result of hate and jealousy. Cain was afraid because of his terrible sin, and he wanted to run away from God as Adam and Eve had once tried to hide from Him.

But God spoke to Cain, saying: "Where is your brother Abel?"

Cain refused to tell what he had done. "I do not know," he lied. "Am I my brother's keeper?"

Cain hoped that God would not know what he had done. He tried to hide his sin by telling a lie. How often when we make a mistake we try to cover it by telling a lie, which is another sin. We cannot hide anything from the Lord; He sees what we do and hears every word we speak.

Cain should have been his younger brother's protector and companion. He should have loved him and guarded him from all harm. God punished Cain for his sin. He told him that he must wander on the earth without friends, for other people would be afraid of him. He would be shunned and despised as a murderer.

Adam and Eve were heartbroken when they found their life-less son. But tears of grief could not bring Abel back to life. The wages of sin is death. They suffered much more because Abel had been killed by his brother. They could see the results of their own sin in the sorrow that came to their home.

Cain did not want to face his parents any longer, so he left home and wandered away to a land called Nod. Adam and Eve were left alone. They missed Cain, and they mourned for Abel. How often they dreamed of the happy days in the Garden of Eden, and they longed to return to that perfect home.

Another son was given to Adam and Eve, and he was named Seth. Other sons and daughters were born to them as the years passed. It is difficult for us to realize how long people lived in those days. Adam was 130 years old when Seth was born. Father Adam was strong, and he lived to see eight generations of children born into the world. Think of nine generations in a family all living at one time! Imagine calling Adam great-great-great-great-great-great-grandfather!

Eve loved her grandchildren, and, no doubt, when they were babies, she thought of God's promise and hoped one of the sons would be the promised Saviour. What thrilling stories Adam could tell Seth, Enoch, Methuselah, and Lamech when they were boys. Father Adam was 874 years old when Lamech, the child of the ninth generation was born. Through the years all of the boys and girls must have listened to Adam's stories of the Garden of Eden and of how he talked with God.

Adam did not die until he was 930 years of age. That is a long time, indeed; but one man, Methuselah by name, lived longer than that.

The FLOOD DESTROYS the EARTH

GENESIS 6-8

AS THE years passed, more and more people lived on the earth. Those who had flocks and herds settled in the green valleys where the rivers flowed. These shepherds lived in tents made from the skins of sheep and goats. They traveled from place to place so that the flocks and herds could have green pastures and plenty of water. Trees, vines, and shrubs made the land beautiful, although it was not as perfect as the Garden of Eden had been.

Men were skillful in their work. They made many tools from brass and iron. They also made harps and other musical instruments for happy hours of entertainment. But they became so wrapped up in their business and pleasure that they forgot God and did not thank Him for food, shelter, and all the good things they had. They made gods of wood and stone and worshiped them. They thought only of themselves and of eating, drinking, and having a merry time. They became lawless in their deeds, killing, stealing, and lying to get the things they wanted. Finally they became so evil that God, who loved His children, declared He was sorry He had created man. What a terrible thing for man, who had been created in the image of God, to fall so low in sin!

© P.P.P.A., N. BRICE, ARTIST

When the ark was ready, the animals came down from the hills and out of the forests.
As the beasts moved forward in a giant parade, the people watched with amazement.

There were a few people who were loyal to God and obeyed His word. Among them was Enoch, the seventh generation from Adam. He probably heard the story of the Garden of Eden from Adam. Although most of the people were selfish and wicked, Enoch was always ready to obey God's word. He "walked with God, and then he disappeared" from the earth. He did not die; he was taken to heaven. Here was a man in a world of sin who lived a pure, honest life. He walked with God on the earth for three hundred years before he was taken to heaven. The son of Enoch was Methuselah, who reached the great age of 969 years. Think of living to be almost a thousand years old! Indeed, he was the oldest man who ever lived.

When the Lord saw the wickedness of man becoming greater and greater, He said: "I will blot the men that I have created off the face of the ground." But then He thought of Noah. Here was a man who also walked with God and obeyed His words. Noah was the great-grandson of Enoch. Noah had a wife and three sons, Shem, Ham, and Japheth. God told this faithful man that the earth was to be destroyed; but that he and his family could be saved. Noah was to make an ark, or giant boat. God told Noah that, when it was finished: "You shall enter the ark, accompanied by your sons, your wife, and your sons' wives."

Faithful Noah believed what God said, and he began work on the mammoth boat. What a strange sight it must have been to watch the building of a boat such as no man had ever made before! It was about six hundred feet long, one hundred feet wide, and sixty feet high. It had three decks, and it was made of strong wood covered with pitch, or tar, inside and out so that it would not leak.

The Lord told Noah to gather food and supplies for his family and for all the animals, for He said that a mighty flood of water would destroy every living creature on the earth.

For one hundred twenty years Noah and his sons worked on the great boat. Many of the people watched the shipbuilders at their work. What is Noah making? they wondered.

Noah told them he was building an ark, as God had commanded. He told them that the earth was to be destroyed by a flood of water. Furthermore, Noah asked his friends to help build the boat and to come on board when it was ready. There would be room for them if they would accept God's invitation.

But the neighbors laughed at Noah, and said he was foolish. They had never seen rain, for until that time the earth had always been watered by a mist that came up out of the ground. As the time drew near when the boat would be finished, Noah begged the people to save themselves from the terrible Flood; but men

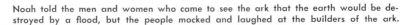

Noah told the men and women who came to see the ark that the earth would be destroyed by a flood, but the people mocked and laughed at the builders of the ark.

W. WILKE, ARTIST

and women refused to believe his warning. They thought the sun would always shine just as it had during their lifetime.

Noah was not discouraged, for he trusted in God. When the ark was finished, the Lord told Noah to take his wife, and his three sons and their wives, and get on board. Once more Noah invited his neighbors to come with him, but they all refused. Then Noah and his family left their home for the last time. The crowd laughed as the eight people walked up the gangplank and entered the ark.

Then a strange thing happened. Out of the forests and down from the hills came the animals. Camels and tigers, bears and elk, lions, giraffes, and wolves moved toward the ark, yet no man was driving them. There was a rush of air as flocks of birds darkened the sky. They flew to the huge boat and found shelter. Two of every kind of bird, beast, and creeping thing came at God's call. Seven pairs of the clean animals, such as the sheep and cattle, which man would need after the Flood, sought safety within the ark.

What a sight it must have been. Here was the most gigantic animal parade the world has ever seen! What a lesson it should have been to those who stood watching! Men would not obey God, but the animals heeded His call. The wicked people looked on with amazement. Perhaps some of them began to worry a bit and wished they had gone with Noah; but no one had the courage to enter the ark.

When all the animals were safely sheltered in the boat, God shut the great door. It did not begin to rain at once. No, for seven days the sun shone. The people on the outside must have laughed at Noah and his family, who were shut up in the

The stormy winds and the huge waves tossed the ark to and fro, but God remembered Noah and his family, and He protected them during the months the Flood raged.

ark. But on the eighth day dark clouds gathered in the sky, the lightning flashed, and the storm broke in terrible fury. Wind drove the rain in great sheets over the land. Day and night the water continued to pour from the sky, and the rivers rose higher and higher. The floodwaters destroyed all the homes built in the valleys, and thousands of people ran to the hills and mountains seeking shelter from the fury of the storm. Some of the wicked people remembered Noah's ark. They pounded on the door; but it could not be opened. They were too late!

Forty days and nights it rained. The ark was lifted by the rising water from the place where Noah had built it, and the waves rocked it to and fro. The ground was broken, and out of giant cracks poured floods of water.

The waves rose higher and higher until the trees, rocks, and hills were covered. Men and women climbed to the tallest mountains, but they could not find a way of escape from the rising waters. The Flood covered all the land, and was at least twenty feet deep above the highest mountain. Every human being and all the animals were destroyed except those who were safe in the storm-tossed boat.

The Flood tore up the surface of the earth. Great rocks tumbled down from the mountains; forests were buried under tons of dirt, and many of the plants and animals were covered by sand and rocks. The buried trees and plants have since been changed into coal. In some of the layers of coal that are dug from mines today can be found fern and leaf patterns showing that they originally came from trees and vegetation.

The mountains and valleys were never again as beautiful as when God created the earth. Scars and gashes made by the torrents of water may still be found on the sides of mountains and in valleys in some parts of the earth. Shells of sea creatures have been dug up on high mountains, thus proving that only a great flood of water could have carried them to these high peaks.

During the storm, what happened to the ark? Noah and his family were safe in the boat, although it was beaten to and fro by the floodwaters. They must have longed for the winds and rain to cease, for the ark tossed and pitched on the stormy seas for five long months. Finally the rain stopped, but the sturdy craft continued to float for weeks. Then a strong wind dried the flood waters, and the mountains appeared once more. Lower and lower dropped the water, until the boat finally settled on the land. How wonderful it was to feel something solid again!

Men and women who had refused to enter the ark now climbed to the highest mountains; even there they could not find a way of escape, for the Flood covered the land.

The day came when Noah decided to send out a raven. If there was dry land, it would find a place to live. The bird flew to and fro, but returned to the boat for refuge, and Noah knew that water still covered the earth. A week later he let a dove fly from the ark; but she also returned. Would the water always cover the earth? the sons of Noah must have asked. Then they remembered God's promise and waited patiently. Another week passed, and Noah sent the dove again. In the evening she returned with the leaf of an olive tree in her beak. There was joy in Noah's family, for now they knew there was dry land once more and that they could soon leave the ark.

Another week passed, and Noah let the dove fly away again. This time she did not come back. Then Noah took the cover off

Noah sent forth the dove from the window, and she returned with an olive leaf in her beak. He knew there was dry land and that they could soon leave the ark.

(77)

Noah built an altar and offered a sacrifice to the Lord. He saw the rainbow—a promise from God that He would never again destroy the earth by a terrible flood.

the top of the ark and looked out. There lay the dry surface of the earth!

"Come out of the ark," God said to Noah. Eight happy people left the boat that had been their home for such a long time. Now they could start life anew in a world that still kept much of its promise of beauty. First of all, Noah built an altar and offered a sacrifice to God for His protection and love. The Lord blessed Noah and his family, and He told them that they would be protected from animals that were growing fierce and dangerous. The wild beasts would now be afraid of man.

As long as the world stood, the Lord said there would be summer, winter, spring, and autumn. This was a blessing, for men could expect the seasons to return at the regular time.

Days came when dark clouds gathered and rain fell on the earth. No doubt Noah and his sons wondered if there would be another flood. But God wanted man to feel safe, so He promised Noah that the world would never again be destroyed by water.

One day after a shower of rain, Shem and Ham pointed to a great colored arch in the heavens. What could it be?

It was a rainbow, and they soon found its meaning, for God said: "I put My rainbow in the clouds, and it shall be a symbol of the covenant between Myself and the world." The rainbow is a message from God always telling men that the earth will not again be destroyed by a flood of water. It is also a promise that someday God will make a new world like the perfect one He created in the beginning.

M. AYER, ARTIST

5

BUILDING the FIRST CITY

GENESIS 10; 11

Busy were the days for Noah and his sons after they left the ark. They must have been glad to work, building homes, plowing fields, planting grain, and making vineyards, for they had been in the boat so long without much to do. Within a few years there were children and strong young folks in the families to help harvest the grain and care for the herds of cattle and the flocks of sheep.

Noah was six hundred years old when he went into the ark, and he lived three hundred fifty years in the new world after the Flood. His children and grandchildren made their homes in the hills near the spot where the ark came to rest; but as families increased in size, they moved to the valleys and plains. Noah told his grandchildren the story of how God saved them from the Flood. He repeated the promise of the coming of the Hero, who would save men from sin and death.

Some of the great-grandsons of Noah did not love God. They forgot how the Creator had brought their family safely through the terrible destruction. All their interest was in cattle and lands, and in becoming powerful leaders. These men traveled to the grassy plains called the land of Shinar. On this plain many families gathered, and they began to build the first cities. Nimrod,

(81)

The people of Babel were proud of the tower they thought would reach heaven.

W. WILKE, ARTIST

a grandson of Ham, was one of these leaders. "He was a mighty hunter," and he established four cities. One of them was Babel, later called Babylon.

In the city of Babel there was excitement one day. "Have you heard the news?" said one shopkeeper. "The leaders are going to build a gigantic tower that will reach to heaven."

"It cannot be done," another answered.

"But the plans are made," came the excited reply.

Yes, the people had decided to build a great tower that would be the talk of all the world. It would reach up toward the heavens, and if another flood came they said they would climb to the top of the tower and be safe. The people of Babel had forgotten God, and they worshiped idols of gold and silver.

Bricks were made of clay and baked in ovens until they were hard. Workers hauled them to the place where the foundations were to be laid. The men labored long hours, and the tower began to rise. Temple rooms for the worship of idols were made in the lower part of it. How proud the people of Babel were! They were building a tower that would bring fame to their city.

One day while the commands were being given to carry brick and mix mortar, a mysterious thing happened. The men could not understand the words the leader was speaking. They were strange new sounds! Up to this time "the whole earth used only one language." But now all was changed! The bricklayers seemed to be babbling as they waved their hands. The men who shouted orders to the stonecutters spoke another language, and the leaders were calling in sounds none of the others could understand. It was as if people speaking Russian, Chinese, Spanish, English, and Dutch all talked in their own language at once.

All was confusion among the builders of the tower. The leaders shouted, but the workers only shook their heads. They could not understand the words that were spoken.

What had happened? Men in their pride had forgotten God, and they thought they could make the world perfect by their own wisdom and strength. So the Creator, who had made man and had given him the power to speak, changed the language of the people. Now they could not understand one another's words.

Work was stopped at once on the Tower of Babel. All was confusion. Some of the leaders were angry, but what could they do? They shouted and clapped their hands, but the workers only shook their heads. The people of one family could not make out what their neighbors said. Soon men and women began to move out of the city of Babel. If they could not tell the shopkeepers what they wanted to buy, they would go and live somewhere else. The few people who spoke the same language traveled together, and soon they were far from Babel. In this way they were scattered abroad from that proud and wicked city, and the tower was never finished.

This is the story of how the different languages had their beginning. God had a purpose in scattering people over the earth. They would be happier and have more to eat and more room if they lived in the country and not in crowded cities. When they refused to obey God's plan, He changed their language, and then they could not live happily when they were crowded together.

The men of Babel did not think that God knew what they were doing when they tried to build the tower. They said they would do as they pleased; it was their business and nobody could stop them. But God looked down from heaven, and He saw the wickedness of their hearts. In a moment of time He changed all their plans because they refused to obey and trust Him.

God sees you and me. He knows if we truly love Him, and if we are willing to follow His rules. He can see the mean look, He can hear the unkind, impure words, and He knows if we try to cheat. If we truly love God and try to do right, He will forgive our mistakes and help us gain the victory over bad words, impure thoughts, and selfish deeds.

Captain Tim's Bible Quiz

NUMBER I

When Captain Tim heard that his three friends, the Barrett youngsters, had been reading the book of Genesis, he told them he would find out what they knew about it. So he picked out some of the important points in the first ten chapters of Genesis. See how well you can answer his questions. The answers are on page 251.

1. Who was the father of Enoch?
2. What did God create on the first day?
3. How many persons were saved in the ark when the Flood destroyed the earth?
4. What was the name of Adam and Eve's first son?
5. Name the oldest man who ever lived.
6. How much higher than the tallest mountain did the waters of the Flood go?
7. What appeared on the fourth day of creation?
8. How was the earth watered before the Flood?
9. When the dove returned to the ark the second time, what did she bring in her beak?
10. Who "walked with God, and then disappeared" from the earth?
11. Upon what mountain did the ark rest after the Flood?
12. Who said: "Am I my brother's keeper?"
13. About how long and how high was the ark?
14. Who named the animals and birds?
15. What creature was used to tempt Eve?
16. Why was the Garden of Eden guarded by an angel after man sinned?
17. Which day of the week is the Sabbath?
18. Into how many rivers was the river of Eden divided?
19. Of what tree were Adam and Eve commanded not to eat?
20. What did Abel bring as a sacrifice to the Lord?

(85)

BURIED CITIES *and* STRANGE WRITING

"I'VE been thinking about the Tower of Babel since I read the Bible story of how it was built, Captain Tim. Have the ruins ever been found?" Dick was chatting with his friend as they sat in the lawn swing in the Lane yard while Bette and Roy played with Chips, the Lane's cocker spaniel. It was a lazy autumn afternoon with warm sunshine and a smoky blue sky.

"Some people believe the place has been found, Dick. I visited the spot with a native guide one time when I was in Mesopotamia. There are some ruins all right, and the natives tell the story that has come down for generations of a great tower that once stood there."

"What happened to it?"

"During the thousands of years since it was built, men have carried away the bricks for houses and temples. It was easier to take them than to make others. Today one sees only a pile of ruins; but I believe the great tower could have been there all right. If it is the place, then it certainly is a lesson to man, telling him that he cannot rise to heaven by his own works."

(87)

The captain and his three young friends saw many ancient treasures at the museum.

J. WILKE, ARTIST

Chips came running with his ball and laid it at his master's feet. The dog was teasing the captain to throw it. Bette and Roy came up to the lawn swing where the captain was sitting. Roy stretched out on the grass, and Bette sat down in the swing beside her friend.

"Chips wore us out, captain," said Bette. "Whew! I don't believe he ever gets tired of running for his ball."

"Lie down, Chips," commanded the dog's owner. "You need to rest, old fellow. You can't play all the time, that's certain."

"We were talking about the Tower of Babel, Roy," explained Dick. Captain Tim tells me that men dig to find the ruins of ancient cities, temples, and towers."

"Yes, indeed," said the man. "It is a great study, and there are scientists who make it their lifework to search for the ruins of

Digging in the ruins of old Babylon, archaeologists have found treasures in the houses and temples which tell us how the people lived three thousand years ago.

ancient cities. The sands of the desert have covered many of these places during the centuries, so scientists go with natives who dig for the treasures of the past."

"Men who do this are called ark—something," said Bette.

"*Archaeologists* is the word," said the captain.

"I'm sure I'll never be one, anyway," responded the girl. "I'm going to be a nurse."

"Were you ever near any of the old cities?" asked Dick of their storyteller.

"Yes, I've been in many of the ancient cities. In fact, I saw the ruins of one of the oldest cities mentioned in the Bible."

"Where was it, Captain Tim?" asked Bette, hoping to get a story from her friend.

"It was the old city of Ur of the Chaldees."

"Isn't that where Abraham lived?" suggested Dick.

"Right you are. Abraham was born there."

"What did the place look like?" put in Roy. "I'd like to see an old city that has been uncovered by archaeologists."

"Ur is only a few miles from the Euphrates River in the land that today is called Iraq. But about four thousand years ago the Chaldeans lived there. Ur was a city of many brick buildings. The bricks were dried in the hot sun, and they made strong houses, for the walls of some of the buildings are still standing. I saw the temple of the moon-god, the largest building in Ur. It was decorated with figures of lions and bulls. They told me that many interesting things were dug from the ruins."

"What were some of them, Captain Tim?"

"Well, Bette, they found a gold helmet, gold axes, cups, and goblets. There were harps and many other carved pieces."

The Chaldean people had strange-looking writing on clay tablets. The writing is called cunei-form. These tablets, buried for ages, have been discovered recently by archaeologists.

"I never knew that those ancient people could make such things!" exclaimed Dick.

"Oh, yes, I forgot to tell you they have found the beautiful jewelry of one of the queens who lived five thousand years ago. There were gold earrings, necklaces, and a head ornament of gold flowers fastened to a comb. There were also necklaces of precious stones," added the man.

"I think I'll be an archaeologist," Roy declared. "It sounds as if one could make a fortune."

"Don't think that the discoverers keep the treasures. They are all put in museums for everyone to see."

"Did people read and write in those days?" asked Dick.

"Certainly, the Chaldean people had writing. It looks strange to us, for the marks are wedge-shaped signs made in soft clay tablets. The writing is called *cuneiform,* meaning 'wedge-shaped.' Some of their words would look like this."

Captain Lane made some marks with his pencil on the top of the newspaper he was holding. The Barrett trio watched him make the drawings. "I'd rather have our language," decided Bette, after looking at the queer signs.

"No doubt you would," said her friend with a laugh. "But remember, these people had libraries with thousands of clay tablets. Some of these have been found which tell the full story of the Flood much like the account in the Bible. In those ancient times people kept records on these tablets of buying and selling land and of the purchase of sheep. Contracts, wills, bills for selling slaves, and thousands of other business records have been discovered. After they wrote on the soft clay with a stick, the clay tablet was baked and became as hard as a brick. Some of the oldest clay tablets have been found at Ur."

"How strange!" exclaimed Roy. "Think of having blocks of clay to read in school."

"Do we know how those people lived? Can you give us any light on that, Captain Tim."

"We know a great deal about the men and women, Dick, although they lived about four thousand years ago. They wrote letters on clay tablets and often put them in clay envelopes with the name of the one to whom it was addressed on the outside. To open the letter, the person who received it had to break off the outside clay."

"I wouldn't have wanted to be a postman in those days. You'd have to carry a load of clay bricks," said Roy with a laugh.

"Some of the people lived in the cities," the captain continued; "but many more lived in tents and roamed around the country with their camels, and their flocks and herds. When the people scattered from the Tower of Babel, some of them settled in the country of the plains and built the city of Ur. Most of these peo-

(Above) A section of the brick wall and one of the gates of ancient Babylon, showing the beautiful designs in the wall.

(Below) One of the figures with wings and a human head which guarded the gates.

BERLIN MUSEUM

LOUV

(Above) A carved tablet showing the king worshiping the sun-god.

(Below) Ruins of the city of Babylon as they have been uncovered by the spades of archeologists.

UNIVERSITY OF PENNSYLVANIA MUSEUM

KEYSTONE

ple worshiped idols carved out of wood and stone, and they built temples to honor the sun and the moon. They had forgotten the true God who made the world."

"Why did they worship the sun and the moon?" asked Bette.

"When they did not believe in the Creator they worshiped the brightest things they saw. The sun gave light and warmth, and seemed to be the source of life, so they worshiped it. Then the moon was beautiful, therefore they called it a god," explained Captain Lane.

"It must have made God very sad to see how His children turned from Him," said Bette.

"I'm sure it did," replied the man. "But God kept loving His world just the same."

"It seems strange that men couldn't learn to obey God after the Flood. That terrible punishment should have been a lesson to everyone that God means what He says." Roy spoke seriously as he stroked the silky ears of Chips.

"It is easy for men to forget God when life goes along smoothly. There were some men who didn't forget Him," went on the captain. "Abram was not a worshiper of idols."

"But didn't God ask him to leave his home in Ur and go to another land?" queried Dick.

"That's exactly what the Bible says. Abram was a son of Terah, who descended from the family of Shem, the son of Noah. Terah was probably a farmer who had herds of cattle and flocks of sheep. He had three sons named Abram, Nahor, and Haran. The boys were kept busy caring for the herds and helping plant the seed and gather the harvest.

"Terah probably worshiped the moon-god in the temple at

Ur. But Abram had heard of the true God who created the earth, and he refused to worship idols of wood or stone. The Lord loved this faithful man and wanted to protect him from the evil ways of the pagan people. Therefore He commanded Abram to leave his home and his family. He asked him to take everything that he owned and begin the journey to a strange land far away."

"It must have taken courage to do that," commented Dick. "I guess Abram was a sort of pioneer, wasn't he, Captain Tim?"

"He was a pioneer for God. That's a good name for him, Dick. And it certainly took courage and faith for him to leave home and relatives to go to a foreign land. But Abram and his wife, Sarah, decided to obey the Lord's command. When he was ready to leave, Terah, his father, went with the caravan. Haran, the brother of Abram, had died; but his son, Lot, ventured on the journey. Abram's other brother, Nahor, joined the caravan."

"How did they travel?" asked Bette.

"They probably rode on camels and donkeys," explained the captain. "Some of the servants drove the cattle and flocks. Their tents and other possessions were carried on four-wheeled wagons or on pack animals. The families made a large caravan and the bells on the pack animals tinkled as they jogged slowly along on their journey."

"I've heard that the camel is called 'the ship of the desert,' " commented Bette.

"Yes, and some persons get sick because of the swaying motion. I remember my first ride," said the captain. "But let's go on with our story. The caravan probably traveled along the river valleys for about three hundred miles until it came to a town called Haran. Old father Terah was ready to settle down when he got there. It had been a long trip for him. Abram stayed with his father until he died at the age of two hundred five years."

"The life of man was getting much shorter. Think of Adam living nine hundred thirty years as compared with Terah living only two hundred five years," said Bette.

"But think of being two hundred years old as compared with the sixty or seventy years people live today," returned Roy.

"Did Abram go on to his promised new home after his father died?" Dick questioned eagerly.

A telephone was ringing in the Lane home. "I'm afraid this will end the story for this time," explained the man. That's probably my wife telling me to meet her downtown. Why don't you go on reading for yourselves? You'll find Abram involved in an exciting kidnaping if you begin reading the twelfth chapter of Genesis. Good-by now." And the genial storyteller limped into the house, carefully protecting his leg.

"I'm going to visit the museum as soon as I get a chance," said Roy, as the trio walked toward the Barrett home.

"So am I," chimed in Bette; "and I'm going to finish reading Genesis."

"I wonder who was kidnaped?" asked Dick thoughtfully, jingling the coins in his pocket.

7

Abram and Lot look out upon the rich valley of the Jordan River. Because of his selfishness, Lot chose the rich lands of the valley near the cities of Sodom and Gomorrah.

6

A SELFISH CHOICE and a KIDNAPING

GENESIS 12:1-14; 13 to 16

WHEN Terah, Abram's father, died in the city of Haran the family wondered what would happen. Would Abram return to the old home in Ur or go on to the strange new country? Soon the brave pioneer received God's command: "Leave your land, your relatives, and your father's home, for the land that I will show you; and I will make a great nation of you."

So one morning the servants were given instructions to load the pack animals and get the carts ready for the journey. When all was ready, the signal was given to start, and the caravan moved out of the city. Abram took with him his nephew, Lot, and his family; but Nahor decided to stay at Haran. It must have been a long parade of camels, donkeys, carts, sheep, and cattle that started south and west from Haran.

It was a dangerous journey, for the hot desert of Syria had to be crossed. Water was scarce in that sandy country, and sometimes, when caravans lost their way, men and animals died of thirst. Then, too, there were thieves along the roads, who hid among the rocks and attacked travelers, robbing them of their possessions. But God protected the caravan of Abram as it moved toward the land of Canaan. After weeks, and perhaps months, of tiresome travel, the pioneer arrived in Shechem. There he found a grove of oak trees and a wide grassy valley— an ideal place to pitch his tents, especially after the dust and heat of the desert. Abram was thankful God had protected his family, his servants, and his flocks and herds; therefore he built an altar at Shechem and made a thank offering to the Lord.

As Abram traveled through the land, he saw streams of water tumbling over the rocks and through the valleys. He saw fields of wheat and barley, grapevines, fig trees, and olive groves. The Lord said to Abram: "To your descendants I am going to give this land." But it seemed like a strange promise to Abram, for he was more than seventy-five years of age, and he and Sarai had no children.

It took a great deal of courage for Abram to believe that God would give him this land, for the people who lived there were fierce fighters, and they did not welcome a stranger any too kindly. But Abram, "the friend of God," talked with the Lord at night under the starry sky, and God repeated the promise that Abram would be the father of a great nation.

Soon the day came when the servants were commanded to load the donkeys and the carts once more. Abram and Lot had decided to move south again. This time they came to Bethel and pitched their tents. Here Abram built another altar to the Lord of heaven.

There came a year when no rain fell. The rivers grew shallow and finally dried up. The herdsmen came to Abram to tell him that the grass was brown and there was little for the sheep and cattle to eat. What should they do to save the flocks and herds from starving? The servants wondered if Abram would leave this land when trouble came to him. Sometimes Abram thought of the old home far off in the land of Ur, but his courage and faith did not fail in this crisis. He decided to take his family to Egypt, where there was plenty of food. They could live in that country where the rich meadowland was watered by the Nile River, until rains made the land of Canaan green once more.

In Egypt Abram met Pharaoh and received gifts from him. But when the famine had ended, the pioneer was anxious to return to Canaan. The caravan traveled back to Bethel, where Abram and Lot again pitched their tents. By this time Abram was very rich in cattle, and in silver and gold. Lot also had many flocks and herds. The animals needed plenty of pasture, and the servants of Abram began to quarrel with the servants of Lot over the best grazing land.

When Abram heard of the trouble, he said to his nephew, Lot: "There simply must be no quarrel between you and me, nor between your herdsmen and mine; for we are kinsmen." Abram loved peace, so he offered the younger man any part of the country he wanted. Instead of giving Abram the first choice, since he was older, Lot looked over the land and selfishly picked the rich Jordan Valley.

Lot made a sad mistake when he moved to this valley. If he had talked the matter over with his uncle, Abram would no doubt have told him not to go there. But Lot was selfish and his love of riches caused him to forget the dangers in that part of the land.

Lot and his family were kidnaped by the fierce kings that attacked the city of Sodom, and the armies started northward taking the captives to be slaves in foreign countries.

In this valley there were two cities called Sodom and Go-morrah. They were noted for their crime and wickedness; but Lot did not think about this. He took his wife and children, his servants, his sheep, his camels, and his gold, and set up his tents near Sodom.

Abram moved to the hills of Hebron, south of Bethel, and pitched his tents under the shady oak trees. He was now a chief in the land, and people knew him to be an honest, unselfish man.

One day a stranger came riding furiously to the camp of Abram. The excited man told how he had just escaped from the armies of four kings who had taken him prisoner. The soldiers of these kings had been fighting in the Jordan Valley, and they had kidnaped the men and women from the cities of Sodom and Gomorrah. Now Lot and his family, and all that he owned had been captured by the enemy, and the soldiers were carrying them away as prisoners. Lot's selfishness had brought him into serious trouble.

Abram quickly called three hundred eighteen of his servants who were trained warriors, and they set out after the enemy, hoping to save Lot and his family. Across the plains and over the hills Abram rode at the head of the troop. Could this band of men fight the armies of the enemy kings and rescue the prisoners? Abram must have thought of this many times. He knew there were grave dangers, but he was not afraid, for his trust was in God.

Day after day Abram and his men pursued the armies. It was not difficult to follow the trail, but would they be able to

As Abram returned victorious in battle he gave a tenth of all the goods to Melchizedek, the priest of the Lord. Abram was blessed because he gave a tithe to God.

ANDRIN, ARTIST

save Lot and his family? Often these fierce kings tortured and killed their prisoners. Although the nephew had been ungrateful and selfish in his dealings with his uncle, Abram forgot all this. He loved Lot and wanted to save him and his family from a terrible fate.

One night Abram's advance guard came upon the enemy. The scouts discovered the camp near the town of Dan. The armies had settled for the night, and the guards were sleepy. Abram divided his troop of warriors into groups, and they surrounded the camp. At the signal to attack, the valiant men rushed forward and surprised the guard. The king of Elam was killed, and the armies fled. Abram's men chased the soldiers until they reached the town of Hobah. Lot and his family, as well as many other prisoners, were soon set free, and all of their possessions were saved. It was a happy reunion, and soon they started a victorious march toward home.

The king of Sodom heard the news, and he rode out to meet Abram's troop of warriors. Grateful that his people had been rescued, the king offered Abram all the treasure that he had captured.

"I would not take anything that belongs to you," said Abram to the king, "not even so much as a thread or a sandal lace, lest you should say, 'It was I who made Abram rich.'"

On the homeward journey Abram met a priest of God named Melchizedek. This good man blessed the brave leader, and Abram gave the priest a tenth of all the goods he had taken. The Lord asks us to give Him a tenth, or tithe, of what we earn. We should be happy to give a tenth to our Creator for the life and health that He gives us. Abram gave God a tenth, and he was blessed and prospered for his faithfulness. Truly Abram loved the Lord with all his heart, and he was the friend of God.

One evening soon after the rescue of Lot, Abram was walking in the cool night air. He was troubled as he thought of the enemy kings, and how they might return and attack him and his family. He knew they were cruel warriors who would seek revenge if only they could. While he was considering this danger, God said: "Do not be afraid, Abram, I am your shield; your reward shall be very great." The man took courage and believed that he would be protected. He also remembered that God said all the land of Canaan would be given to his family.

Abram was almost ninety years old, and he had no children. He wondered how his family could possess all the land from Egypt to the Euphrates—a distance of almost five hundred miles—if he had no sons or daughters. God said: "Now look at the sky, and count the stars if you can. So shall be your descendants." While the Lord talked with Abram, He also told him that someday his descendants would go to a strange land where they would be slaves for hundreds of years; but the time would come when they would return to their own country, Canaan.

When Abram was ninety-nine years old, the Lord told him he should have a new name. "Your name shall no longer be called Abram, but your name shall be Abraham; for I am making you the ancestor of a company of nations." Abram meant an "honored father," while Abraham was a name with greater significance, meaning, "father of a multitude." Sarai's name was changed to Sarah, "the princess of the multitude."

7

THREE VISITORS *on a* STRANGE MISSION

GENESIS 18; 19

ONE day about noon Abraham was sitting in the doorway of his tent when he saw three strangers coming up the road. They looked tired and dusty. Abraham was always ready to welcome visitors, so he hurried out to meet the men, and he bowed before them.

"Please do not pass by without stopping with your servant," Abraham said. "Let a little water be brought to wash your feet, and stretch yourselves out under the tree, while I fetch a bit of food that you may refresh yourselves. Afterward you may proceed on your way, since you will then have paid your servant a visit."

"Do as you propose," the men replied, accepting the kindness of their host.

According to the custom of the country, Abraham brought a basin of water, and the men removed their sandals and washed their feet. Then he commanded that food be cooked quickly for his guests. Sarah baked barley cakes, and Abraham had servants prepare meat, butter, and milk. The meal was served to the men as they sat in the shade of an oak tree.

(105)

As Abraham talked with the strangers, he found that he was entertaining visitors from heaven. The Lord and two of His angels had been welcomed by this hospitable man. No wonder Abraham was called "the friend of God." After the travelers had eaten, they arose and started on the road toward Sodom. Abraham walked with them a short distance to see them safely on their journey.

"Shall I hide what I am about to do from Abraham," the Lord said, "seeing that Abraham is bound to become a great and powerful nation? No, I will make it known to him."

What startling news was Abraham about to hear? He listened anxiously for the next words. Sodom and Gomorrah were cities filled with crime and wickedness, said the Lord. Because the people had rebelled against heaven, the Lord was going to visit the cities to see what should be done to them. Abraham was worried when he heard this. He knew the cities were very wicked, and he thought at once of Lot and his family who had moved to Sodom.

Two of the visitors hurried on toward the city, but the Lord remained to talk with His friend. Abraham drew near and said: "Wilt Thou really sweep away good along with bad? Suppose there are fifty good men in the city, wilt Thou really sweep it away, and not spare the place for the sake of the fifty good men that are in it?"

So the Lord said: "If I find in Sodom fifty good men, within the city, I will spare the whole place for their sake."

Then Abraham thought for a moment. How many good persons did he know in Sodom? Lot was a good man, but how many others were there? He was afraid there were not fifty.

ot and his daughters hurried to escape;
is wife was left behind—a pillar of salt.

Abraham asked if the Lord would save the cities if only forty-five good persons could be found. The Lord agreed to this request. But Abraham would not stop there. He persisted in trying to save the cities. Would God spare them if there were forty good men? Yes, was the reply. If there were thirty? Yes, was again the answer. If there were only ten good persons? Once more the Lord agreed to save the cities of the plain even for ten good persons.

Truly Abraham knew how to talk with his Creator. Under the starry heavens the man had prayed many times for faith and courage. Now he could plead with the Lord to spare these wicked cities if there were only ten good men in them, and the Lord agreed to his request. When the Lord had finished speaking, He told his friend good-by and went on His way, and Abraham returned to his tents.

That evening the two angels arrived at the gates of the city of Sodom. Lot was one of the city leaders, and it was the custom for them to sit at the gate to help settle disputes and to act as judges. On this afternoon Lot was sitting at the gate, ready to offer hospitality to strangers. In his polite manner Lot welcomed the two visitors, and urged them to go home with him for the night. They accepted Lot's invitation, and he prepared a feast and they ate.

The wicked men of Sodom heard that strangers had arrived in town, and they surrounded Lot's home. The mob planned to hurt the visitors if they could lay hands on them. They began beating down the door of the house, and soon there would have been serious trouble. But the angels struck the mob with blindness, and then they could do no harm.

When Lot saw what had happened, he knew that his guests were angels. Then the visitors gave him their message. This was the last night for the men and women of Sodom, the angels said, for the city was to be destroyed.

Lot hurried out to warn his children, but his sons-in-law laughed and mocked him. They thought he was joking, for they did not think anything would happen to their proud city. No, there were not fifty persons in Sodom who loved God and believed His word. There were not twenty or ten such faithful men. Therefore, the Lord could not spare the wicked city; but He did save those who were willing to obey His instructions.

Lot must have talked long and earnestly with his wife and his daughters that night, telling them of the terrible fate that awaited Sodom. Early the next morning the angels urged Lot to get out of the city. "Take away your wife and the two daughters that are at hand," said the guests, "lest you be swept away in the punishment of the city."

But it was hard for them to say good-by to their home and their friends. Lot thought of his wealth, and his wife remembered her friends. The husband and wife stood at the door of the house without making any move to leave. Finally the angels could wait no longer. They took Lot's wife and his daughters by the hand and led them to the gates of Sodom.

"Fly for your life," cried the angels; "do not look behind you." Time was short, for the doomed city was about to be destroyed.

The frightened family hurried along the road leading out of the valley. Don't look back, don't look back! The words rang in their ears. But Lot's heart was still in Sodom, and Lot's wife remembered her friends and her relatives. The daughters thought of the parties and gay times they had enjoyed. Don't look back! Again the words echoed in their ears.

Then Lot's wife hesitated. She would look back! Besides, it was foolish for them to hurry and leave, she thought. Instead of being thankful, she was angry. She would see if anything was happening to Sodom. She refused to obey God's rules. As she turned and looked back, something dreadful happened. She turned into a pillar of salt. What a strange monument to disobedience! There in the valley by the roadside stood a statue of salt—Lot's wife, a fearful symbol of what it costs to disobey the Lord's commands.

Lot and his two daughters hurried on to the little city of Zoar. As the morning sunshine came over the hills they entered the gates of the town.

What was happening in Sodom? Men and women began to go about the streets as usual that morning. There was business in the markets where men bought and sold their goods. The sons-in-law of Lot who had refused to go with him laughed as they thought of the man and his family hurrying away from the city.

Suddenly out of the clear sky there came an explosion of fire! Sulphur and flames fell upon Sodom and Gomorrah. The palaces and temples, the merry throngs of wicked people, the homes and gardens—all were destroyed! Smoke rolled up in the sky as if a giant furnace were blazing.

Abraham arose early that morning and looked down the road toward Sodom. He was anxious to know if the Lord had found ten good men in Sodom and Gomorrah. Then he saw

Abraham arose early and looked toward Sodom. When he saw the smoke rising higher and higher from the plain he knew God had not found ten good people in the cities.

the smoke! It rose higher and higher in black clouds. The cities were being destroyed. Abraham knew that there had not been ten people in Sodom and Gomorrah who would obey the God of heaven. Later he was to learn that the angels had been able to save only Lot and his wife and their two daughters from the wicked cities of the Jordan Valley, and even Lot's wife had come to a tragic end because she disobeyed.

ABRAHAM'S TWO SONS

GENESIS 16; 21

ABRAHAM and Sarah trusted in God, but they often wondered how it would be possible for their family to own the land of Canaan, seeing they had no children. One day Sarah suggested to her husband that he should follow the custom of some of the people and marry another wife. She told him that her maid, Hagar, would be a good wife. Hagar was an Egyptian woman who had been with Abraham's family for ten years since they left Egypt. She had learned to love and worship the true God. So Abraham accepted Sarah's plan and married Hagar. But two wives in the home did not bring happiness. Hagar and Sarah quarreled, and one day the maid was so unhappy she ran away into the desert.

Where shall I go? What shall I do? These were the questions that worried Hagar as she stumbled along the hot, dusty road. She wanted to go back to Egypt, but it was a long way to travel across the desert. Finally she found a fountain of water by the side of the road, and here she stopped to rest. An angel came to her and said: "Hagar, maid of Sarah, where have you come from, and where are you going?"

"I am running away from my mistress Sarah," was all the maid could say, for she did not know where she was going.

(113)

There was no more water in the waterskin, and the sun beat down on Ishmael and his mother.

. CAZIN, ARTIST

Then the angel told her that it was her duty to go back to Abraham's home. Hagar obeyed the angel and returned to her work of serving Sarah faithfully; but life was not pleasant for her. After a time a son was born to Hagar, and he was named Ishmael. Now Abraham was happy, for he could see how his children might some day possess the promised land. As the lad grew to be a strong youth, he loved to shoot with the bow and arrow.

When Ishmael was fourteen years old, another son was born to Abraham while he lived at Gerar, not far from the land of Egypt. This was the son that had long been promised to Sarah and Abraham. They named the baby, Isaac, which means "laughter," and the father, who was now a hundred years old, took great pride in the baby. When Isaac grew older, he played with Ishmael. Abraham made a feast for Isaac when he was old enough to walk. It must have been a happy day for friends and neighbors who came to celebrate with the parents. But the happiness was soon spoiled, for Sarah noticed that Ishmael teased young Isaac. This made the mother very angry. She went to her husband at once and demanded that Ishmael and his mother, Hagar, be sent from the home.

What was Abraham to do? He loved Ishmael, his son, and he did not want to send Hagar away. But there would be no peace in his tents with hatred between Hagar and Sarah. So Abraham prayed, and the Lord told him that it was best for Ishmael and his mother to leave. "It is through Isaac that you are to have descendants bearing your name," God told His friend. Then the Lord said of Ishmael: "I will make a nation of him, too, because he is your child."

Early next morning Abraham called Hagar and told her she must take her son and leave his home. He gave her some food and a waterskin. A waterskin is a bag made from the hide of an animal. The peoples of the East carry water in waterskins when they travel. Abraham told Ishmael and Hagar good-by, and with sadness in his heart he watched mother and son start off on the road that led into the desert.

Hagar trudged along the rough road, and after a while she realized that she was lost. There was no more water in the waterskin, and the hot sun of the desert beat down upon them. Ishmael grew thirsty and tired. At last he could go no farther, so his mother laid him under a bush and went and sat down a little way off. "I cannot bear to see the child die!" she cried.

God was watching over them, and soon an angel came to her. "What is the matter with you, Hagar? Fear not; for God has heard the boy's cry, even here where he is. Come, pick up the boy, and hold fast to him; for I am going to make a great nation of him."

The woman brushed the tears from her eyes and looked about her. Then she stood up and looked again. What did she see? Not far away was a well of water! Quickly she ran to the well, filled the waterskin, and carried a cool drink to her son. Soon Ishmael and his mother were able to go on their journey. They made their home in the desert, and Ishmael grew to be a strong man, skillful in hunting with the bow and arrow.

He married a woman from Egypt, and his twelve sons were warriors in the desert. They lived in tents and traveled from place to place with their flocks. Their descendants are Arabians, who live in the desert country to this day.

9

ABRAHAM'S GREATEST TEST

GENESIS 22; 23

IF YOU have a friend who always keeps his word, you know he can be depended on if you are in trouble. Abraham had found God to be such a friend. We remember that the brave pioneer left his home in Ur and traveled to a strange country when God called him. There had been famine and war, but the Lord had protected His friend in time of danger. Abraham had been greatly blessed, and now he was living at Beersheba, where thousands of his sheep fed on the grass-covered hills, and hundreds of servants and their families dwelt in tents. We remember, too, that Abraham followed the Lord's instructions when there was trouble in his home. Although he was sorry to send Ishmael and Hagar away, he believed God knew best.

Abraham had lived more than a hundred years, but there was no time when the Lord had failed to keep His promise to His friend. Now his greatest happiness was in being with his son Isaac, who had grown to be a strong young man. Abraham depended on him to help run the business and to deal with the servants. The father knew that if the son was to possess the land of Canaan as God had said, he must become a strong, dependable leader.

(117)

The servants waited with the pack animal while Abraham and Isaac climbed the mountain.

W. WILKE, ARTIST

One night while the pioneer stood watching the stars in the blue sky, the Lord spoke to him again. "Abraham!" He said.

"Here am I," said faithful Abraham. Now this time he was given the strangest and saddest message he had ever heard.

"Take your son," said the Lord, "your only son, whom you love, Isaac, and go to the land of Moriah, and there offer him as a burnt offering on one of the hills which I shall designate to you."

Abraham could not understand this command. He had trusted God through all his life, and surely He would not fail him now. But why would the Lord ask him to do such a terrible thing? Wasn't Isaac the son that was to inherit the promised country of Canaan? If he was killed, how would Abraham's family ever possess the beautiful land?

Early in the morning Abraham awakened Isaac and two of his servants and told them they were to make a trip with him to offer sacrifices. Isaac had often gone with his father to worship God, so he was not surprised to be awakened for such a journey. The servants chopped wood and tied it in bundles on a donkey. There were no matches in those days, so it was probably necessary to carry the coals of fire in a pot.

The father and son set out on their journey to the land of Moriah, the place where the city of Jerusalem would someday be built. They did not awaken Sarah to tell her good-by, for Abraham was afraid if he told his wife the sad news, she would stop him from obeying God. The land of Moriah was about fifty miles from the home in Beersheba, and it was not until the morning of the third day of travel that Abraham saw the mountain where he was to make the sacrifice.

The hour of greatest test had come to Abraham, and he was willing to obey God's command. Isaac lay bound upon the altar and the father raised his knife to sacrifice his son.

When they came to the foot of the mountain, Abraham told his servants to stay there with the donkey. Pointing to the mountaintop, the father said: "I and the boy go yonder to perform our devotions, after which we shall return to you." The servants waited with the pack animal, and the father and son began climbing the mountain together. Isaac carried the heavy bundle of wood, while his father carried the knife and the fire.

Noticing that they had no lamb to offer on the altar, Isaac stopped. He thought his father had forgotten to bring a sacrifice. "Father!" said Isaac to his father, Abraham.

"Yes, my son," Abraham responded.

"Here are the fire and the wood," he said, "but where is the sheep for a burnt offering?"

Then Abraham saw a ram caught by his horns in the bushes. He took the animal to the altar, and with true thankfulness offered it as a sacrifice to the Lord for sparing his son.

"God will provide Himself with the sheep for a burnt offering, my son," said Abraham. Then the father and the son started on their climb once more. Abraham did not have the heart to tell Isaac, until it was absolutely necessary, that he was to be the sacrifice.

Finally the father and son came to the place where the altar was to be built. They gathered stones and piled them to make the altar. The wood was carefully arranged on the stones. Then, when there was nothing more to prepare, Abraham told Isaac of God's command. The strong young man listened to his father and was willing to obey and to be the sacrifice. He could easily have run away if he had wanted to; but, no, he allowed his father to lay him on the altar and to tie his hands and feet.

The hour of greatest test had come to Abraham. He knew that the people who worshiped the sun-god in the land of Ur sometimes offered their children as sacrifices to idols, but the true God had never made such a terrible request before. But in this moment Abraham did not disobey God. He lifted the knife to kill his son.

But as his hand was ready to strike, a voice called from heaven: "Abraham, Abraham!"

"Here am I," he replied.

"Do not lay hands on the boy," He said, "do nothing of the sort to him; for I know now that you revere God, in that you have not withheld your son, your only son, from Me."

The father could have shouted for joy. His son was safe! Abraham's love and loyalty to God had been severely tested, but he had proved true.

Then Abraham saw in the bushes a ram caught by his horns. So the father took the animal and offered it as a sacrifice to the Lord. And he called the name of the place Jehovah-jireh, which means: "The Lord will provide."

It was a happy father and son who went down the mountain trail together and met the waiting servants. Soon they were on their way home to Beersheba. Young Isaac must have realized as never before that God had a work for him to do, for his life had been wonderfully spared.

The SEARCH for a BRIDE

GENESIS 23 to 25:9

ONCE more Abraham moved his family, his flocks, and his herds. He left Beersheba to return to Hebron, where the spreading oak trees had given cooling shade for his tents years before. It was near Hebron that Abraham had settled when he and Lot parted. It was here that the Lord and two angels visited the faithful pioneer; and it was here, too, that Isaac had been born. Truly the man was returning to a place of happy experiences.

But now Hebron was to have sad memories for Abraham. Sarah, who had left the home in Ur and traveled with her husband to the land of Canaan, died. As a loyal wife she had gone with Abraham to Egypt in time of famine; she had stood with her husband before kings and princes. She had been the mother of Isaac, as God had promised. And now, at the age of one hundred twenty-seven years, she passed to her rest. Abraham wished to bury his wife in the Cave of Machpelah, which was near Hebron, so he went to Ephron, the Hittite, the owner of the land where the cave was located, and bought the field. When the purchase was completed, Abraham buried his wife in the cave.

As the years passed, this faithful friend of God grew old and feeble. He gave all his property to Isaac and asked him to take

One day Abraham called his oldest and most trusted servant, Eliezer, and told him to take camels and go to Haran to find a wife for his son Issac from among his own people.

charge of the cattle, the sheep, and the other possessions. The son was now forty years of age, but he had never married. Abraham had warned his son that people of Canaan worshiped idols, and he told Isaac he was never to marry a daughter of the neighboring families. But where was Isaac to find a wife? This worried Abraham, for he longed to see his son have a home of his own with children who would possess the great country God had promised them.

One day Abraham thought of a plan to get a wife for Isaac. He called his eldest and most trusted servant, Eliezer, and gave him an important mission. He said: "You will go to my own land and kindred to get a wife for my son Isaac."

"Suppose the woman is unwilling to follow me to this land; am I to take your son back to the land that you left?"

Since the journey required many weeks of travel, Isaac could not go, for he must direct the business. But most of all, Abraham did not want his son to go back to the old home country because Isaac might be tempted to stay there among idol worshipers. Therefore the father said to Eliezer: "See to it that you do not take my son back there! It was the Lord, the God of the heavens, who took me from my father's home and the land of my birth, who spoke to me and made me this promise, 'It is to your descendants that I am going to give this land'—it is He who will send His angel ahead of you, so that you shall get a wife for my son there."

If the woman he should choose for Isaac's wife was unwilling to come back with him, then the servant was released from his special duty. "Only you must never take my son back there," the father warned again.

Ten camels were made ready for the caravan. The animals were fastened together, one behind another, to form a line. Tied to their harness were bronze bells that tinkled as the camels moved. Servants filled sacks with food. It is a long journey, they said, and we must have plenty to eat. Then, into strong bags Eliezer put precious gifts which were to be presents for the girl he would find. The camels were made to kneel, and the bags were loaded on their backs. When the camel train was ready, Eliezer gave the signal to his fellow servants, and they started the camels forward on the road leading northward toward the land of Mesopotamia.

Days and weeks passed before the caravan arrived one afternoon at the gates of the city of Haran. Eliezer made the camels kneel beside the town well where the women came to draw

water in the evening. The hour of test had come. How would
the servant know which of the young women he should choose?

Eliezer believed in the Lord, and he prayed for help. "O
Lord, the God of my master Abraham," he said, "pray give me
success today, and so be gracious to my master Abraham. Here
I am taking my stand beside the spring, as the daughters of the
townsmen come out to draw water. Let the girl, then, to whom
I say, 'Will you please let down your pitcher for me to drink?'
and who says, 'Drink, and let me water your camels as well'—
let her be the one whom Thou hast allotted to Thy servant Isaac.
By this I shall be assured that Thou wilt really be gracious to
my master."

Before he had finished his prayer, a beautiful young woman
came to the well carrying a clay pitcher on her shoulder. She
stepped down to the fountain, filled her pitcher, and was coming up the steps when Eliezer ran to her and said: "Will you
please let me drink a little water from your pitcher?"

The young woman took her clay pitcher, filled it with water from the well, and carried it
to the trough to give the camels a drink. While she did this, Eliezer looked on in silence.

A. CABANEL, ARTIST   KEYSTO

"Drink, sir," she said, and quickly lowering the pitcher to her hand, she gave him a drink. Then she said: "For your camels, too, I will draw water, until they finish drinking." When camels are thirsty, they drink a great deal of water, and the girl must have carried her pitcher many times from the well to the watering trough.

While the young woman was doing this good deed, Eliezer looked on in silence. He saw his prayer was being answered before his eyes! When the camels had finished drinking, the man took a gold ring and two golden bracelets from his bag of treasures and gave them to the maiden. Then he asked: "Whose daughter are you? Pray tell me. Is there room in your father's house for us to spend the night?"

The young woman told him her name was Rebekah, and that she was the daughter of Bethuel, the granddaughter of Nahor, Abraham's brother. "We have plenty of both straw and fodder," she added, "and there is also room to spend the night." Then the servant thanked God for answering his prayer. The girl ran home and told her mother of the guest who had given her beautiful gifts of gold.

Her brother, Laban, saw the rich treasures, and he ran to the well and found Eliezer beside his camels. He welcomed the man. "Come in, you blessed of the Lord," he said. "Why do you stand outside, when I have the house ready, as well as a place for the camels?"

After the camels had been unloaded and fed, Eliezer and his companions were given water to wash their feet, and food was set before them. But Eliezer pushed the food aside, saying: "I will not eat until I have told my story."

9

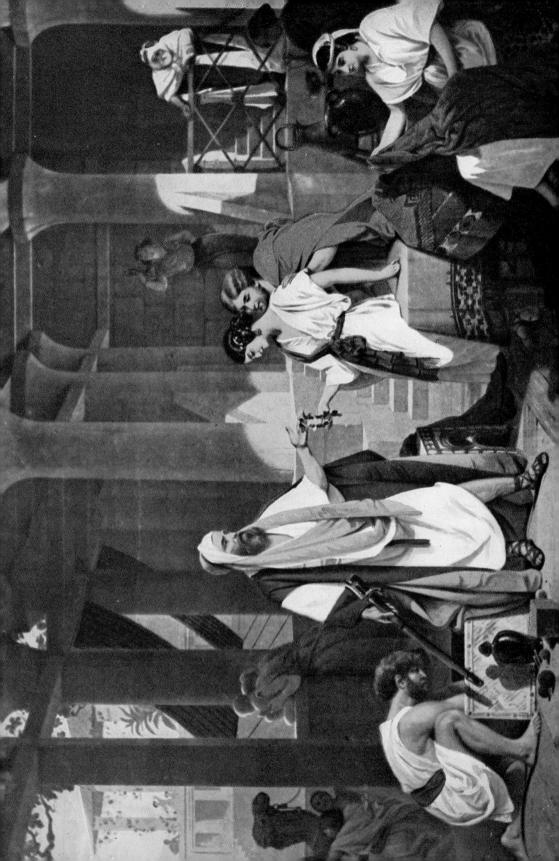

"Say on," said Laban, anxious to know the man's business.

Abraham's servant began by telling of his master's riches and of his son. Then he explained why he had been sent on this long journey. He was to find a bride for Isaac. When he said this he must have looked at Rebekah, and the girl must have known what he meant. He told how he arrived at the city of Haran that afternoon, and how he had prayed that the woman who came to the well and offered him a drink of water, and who gave water to the camels, might be the one who should be the bride for Isaac. While the family listened, Eliezer told how Rebekah came to the well and gave him a drink of water from her pitcher, and then gave water to his camels. The answer to his prayer had been so remarkable that Eliezer said: "I bowed in homage to the Lord, blessing the Lord, the God of my master Abraham, who had led me by the right road to get the daughter of my master's kinsman for his son. Now then, tell me whether you are ready to treat my master kindly and honorably or not, so that I may turn one way or the other."

The family were amazed at the story, and Laban answered: "This is the Lord's doing; we dare not answer you adversely or favorably. Here is Rebekah for you; take her and go; let her become the wife of your master's son, as the Lord has signified."

When Abraham's servant heard these words, he again thanked God for His blessings. Then he opened his box of treasures and brought out gifts of silver and gold for Rebekah. He also gave her many beautiful garments. Then presents were given to her mother and to her brother, Laban. When this had been done, Eliezer and his men ate and drank and stayed at the home that night.

liezer opened his box and gave many gifts of
ilver and gold to Rebekah and to her family.

RAMSTORFF, H. SCHOPIN, ARTIST

The next morning Eliezer awakened his companions, and they prepared the caravan for the journey back to Hebron. Eliezer was anxious to get started, so he said to Rebekah's mother and brother: "Let me go to my master."

But the family did not like to see Rebekah go away from home so soon. The mother thought of the time needed to get Rebekah's clothes ready for the journey and also for her wedding. Therefore they said: "Let the girl stay with us a while longer, or at least ten days, after which she may go."

"Do not hinder me," he said to them; "since the Lord has brought my errand to such a successful issue, let me go that I may return to my master."

"We will call the girl, and consult her wishes," they said. So they called Rebekah, and said to her: "Will you go with this man?"

"I will," she bravely replied.

Quickly the animals were loaded, and Rebekah said good-by to her family. The caravan started, and the girl and her maidens rode away on the camels toward a new home and a husband she had never seen. Eliezer thanked God for answering his prayer and making his mission a success.

While all this was happening, Isaac was in the tents at Hebron. He had not forgotten that Eliezer had gone to find him a bride. Each day he thought of the caravan and wondered if his servant was having success in his mission. One evening as the shadows grew long under the oak trees, Isaac went for a walk in the field. He was thinking of the bride who might be traveling to him, and he prayed that God would guide and bless her.

Listen! In the still evening air he heard the tinkle of bells

People of the desert travel by camel caravans today as they did in Abraham's day. Here we see a bride seated on a camel ready to start on the journey to her future home.

and knew that a caravan was near. They sounded like the bells of his camels. Isaac looked across the field and saw the caravan coming toward him. Yes, they were his camels! Eliezer was coming home.

Now Rebekah saw a man hurrying across the field. She asked Eliezer: "Who is the man yonder that is walking through the fields toward us?"

"He is my master," replied the servant.

The young woman stopped her camel, commanded it to

The young woman, who had traveled for many days with the caravan, stopped her camel and dismounted when she saw the man coming toward her. Eliezer presented her to Isaac.

kneel, and she dismounted. She took a veil and covered herself, as was the custom of the country. When Isaac came near, his servant told him all that had happened and how the Lord had blessed him in finding the maiden. Eliezer then presented Rebekah to his master.

As the crimson sunset lighted the sky, the girl and Isaac walked across the field together toward the tents of Abraham. Isaac heard Rebekah speak to him, and her words blended with the tinkle of the camel bells. In the soft evening light Isaac could see that his bride was beautiful, and he knew from the story Eliezer had told him that she was kind and thoughtful to others. He was thankful that Rebekah had been brave enough to come on the long journey to a strange land to be his wife.

The couple were married, and Isaac loved his wife. He was no longer lonely as he had been after the death of his mother.

There were years of happiness for Abraham, and for Isaac and Rebekah. When Abraham was one hundred seventy-five years old, he died. The pioneer had been a friend of God all his life. Ishmael heard of his father's death, and he came from his desert home to attend the funeral. The two sons, Isaac and Ishmael, buried their father in the Cave of Machpelah, where Sarah had been laid to rest.

QUEER CUSTOMS of LONG AGO

"THERE isn't a more perfect time to take a walk by the river than in the autumn," Captain Timothy Lane was saying to the Barrett trio as they made their way along the path through the wild blackberry vines that grew along the river. "Look at those leaves. It looks as if each one had been hand-painted in rich colors of red, brown, or scarlet."

"The river is lazy," said Bette. "It moves along as if it were tired."

For two weeks Captain Lane had been planning to go on a promised hike with the twins, Bette and Roy, and Dick, their elder brother. But the days had been cold and rainy, making it necessary to postpone the plans again and again. Now the skies had cleared, and a breeze had dried the ground quickly. This afternoon was ideal for a walk to the old mill about a mile down the river. After school the three Barrett youngsters had called promptly for their friend, and now the four of them were on their way with Chips, the brown cocker spaniel, as their mascot.

"Look at that dog run!" called Roy, as Chips bounded through piles of red and brown leaves.

"Maybe he's found the scent of a rabbit," suggested Dick, throwing a rock at a tin can perched on a fence post.

(135)

"This mill was erected here by the river to grind the farmer's grain," said Captain Lane.

N. WILKE, ARTIST

"It's more likely a woodchuck," the captain replied, as he watched the dog burrow into the leaves. "I wish I had half as much ambition to move leaves on my lawn as Chips has to dig them out of that hole."

"Last year I found an arrowhead over by that tree, Captain Tim." Roy pointed toward a large oak tree near the bluff.

"That's interesting, Roy. I'm not surprised, either; for I understand that a number of Indian relics have been found near here. This valley was one of the camping grounds for Indians."

"The first white settlers built a mill here, didn't they?" asked Dick. The four hikers had pushed ahead on the path and were rounding a bend where they could see the old water mill.

"Yes," returned the captain. "I believe a village was built on the bank of this river, and a small mill to grind wheat and corn for the farmers was soon started. Later the son of the first miller erected the mill you see yonder." The man pointed with his cane toward the gray, weather-beaten building that stood as a landmark in the valley.

"Come here, Chips," called Bette, not forgetting the dog, that had stayed behind digging in the leaves. Soon a ball of brown fur with flapping ears, like a pair of wings, was seen as the dog jumped through the tall grass toward his master.

"How did they grind the wheat, Captain Tim?" the girl questioned as they walked up the path to the door of the mill.

"There were two big flat stones, Bette. The top one turned and it had a funnellike hole into which the grain was poured. As the stone turned, the wheat was ground between the two heavy stones."

"Was that all there was to making flour?"

"No, Roy," continued the man. "It was sometimes sifted through cloth to separate the finer grades of flour. But all of it was much coarser than our white flour today, and perhaps it was better food, too."

Dick was looking around the dusty corners of the empty, deserted room. He opened the doors of cupboards, and several spiders scurried out of hiding. "An Indian mill to grind corn was found in a cave not far from here," he was saying as he closed the squeaky doors.

"Yes, I saw it at the city hall. It was an old hand mill used by

Women of Palestine grind the wheat by hand in a stone mill as has been done for generations. Grain is poured into a hole in the top stone and ground between the stones.

THREE LIONS

Some of the dishes and utensils found in the ruins of ancient cities of Palestine. Rebekah may have used such dishes and the stone grinding mill to prepare food for her family.

the Indian women," commented the captain. "In fact, the mill was much like those used in early Bible times. There was a stone with a cuplike hollow in its surface, and a second rock, ball-shaped with a part sticking out to form a handle. Grain was put in the hollow stone to be rolled and mashed by the ball-shaped stone. I've seen women using those little mills in Palestine to grind their grain."

Bette had found a porch overlooking the river, and a comfortable bench where she and the captain could sit while they watched the water pour over the old water wheel. Dick dropped rocks into the stream, and Roy adjusted his camera to take a picture of the river tumbling over the rocks.

"Do you suppose that Abraham's wife made flour in a little stone mill?" queried the girl of her friend.

"It would surely seem so, for that is the way it was done for more than three thousand years in Bible lands." Captain Lane tapped the floor with his cane. "I imagine Sarah took barley or wheat, put it in the stone, and ground the flour. She baked it in a simple way, much like our methods of cooking when we go camping."

"What strange customs they had in those times compared with our way of living today," put in Dick. "I've been reading the story of Abraham and Isaac this week, captain."

"We've all been reading the Bible," added Bette.

"Good for you. There is much to learn in the Book of books." As the captain spoke he settled back comfortably, resting in the warm sunshine.

"Why did Abraham live in tents?" questioned Roy, putting his camera in the case after taking the picture.

"In the land of Ur, where he first lived, he and Sarah probably had a brick house, for we know there were many one-and two-story houses in that city. But they were willing to leave all of this when God called them. When Abraham arrived in Canaan, he lived in tents because it was easy to move from one place to another where the pasture was the best for the sheep and cattle. I've seen many of the tents of the nomads of today which are much like those used in the time of Abraham. The tents are dark brown or black in color and are made of goat's hair. The women weave the goat's hair on small looms. As a family grows in size, the tents can be made bigger to take care of the children."

"I should think the tents would be hot in the daytime," suggested Roy.

"They are in the hot countries," went on Captain Lane. "That was no doubt why Abraham was sitting in the door of his

In Abraham's day the women cooked the food outdoors. Here we see a woman of the desert preparing this sheet of dough to bake on the hot rocks over the fire.

tent at noon on the day the three heavenly guests came to visit him. It was the custom to rest in the shade at the door of the tent in the middle of the day."

"I can understand, too, why Abraham liked the grove of oak trees near Hebron. It would give cool shade for the tents." As Dick spoke he pushed a stick out into the little whirlpool and watched the water toss it about.

"How did Sarah cook the meals for Abraham?" asked Bette, who enjoyed learning to cook in her mother's kitchen.

"She had such simple utensils, I'm afraid you would hardly know how to cook with them, Bette. The stove was probably a few stones set up outside the tent. She had a jar of water and a few pots and pans. To make bread, Sarah would take some of the flour she had ground, mix it with water in a kneading bowl, and make flat cakes. Then she put them on hot stones by the fire to bake. The crisp brown bread could be eaten with fresh butter, milk, or cheese."

"You'll make me hungry," exclaimed Roy. "Be careful, for it's a long time until we eat."

The sun had dipped behind the trees on the west bank of the river, and the suggestion of eating caused the captain to say: "Perhaps we'd better start on the road home. We don't want to be late for dinner."

"But I'm not through asking questions," protested Bette.

"Let's talk as we go along," said Roy.

THREE LIONS

the villages of Palestine there is usually public well where all the women go to pitchers of water for their homes.

"Come, Chips," called the captain. "We're going home, old fellow."

"I wouldn't like to get married like Rebekah did," said Bette, thinking of Abraham's servant going in search of a wife for Isaac.

"Customs are different in those lands, Bette," explained the man who had traveled through Palestine and other countries of the Near East. "The parents often select the husband for a girl, and perhaps the bride has never seen her husband until the day of their marriage."

"Rebekah could at least choose to go or stay." Roy expressed his opinion as the four pushed through the thick bushes growing over the path.

"I think she was brave to go to a strange land to marry a man she had never seen."

"That's right," said the captain. "She believed God was guiding."

The four hikers left the river path and walked along the street toward home. Bette turned to her friend and said: "Captain Tim, why did Rebekah go out to the well to get a pitcher of water?"

"It was the only place to get water in the town, Bette. There was no running water piped to the houses in those days. All the water was drawn from public wells. In Haran, where Rebekah lived, the women carried the big pitchers or jars on their shoulders. It was the custom for the women to go to the well for fresh cool water at the time of the evening meal. It was natural for Eliezer to wait there when he arrived, for he would see most of the women of the town who came to get water.

"Wells were valuable possessions in that dry country," the storyteller went on. "Water was precious, and many times when the streams dried up there was little water for the cattle. Sometimes there were quarrels and fights over wells. When one man dug a well another man might try to take it from him."

"Didn't Abraham have trouble over a well?" asked Roy.

"That's right, Roy. Abraham and Isaac both had trouble getting water for their cattle. Abraham made a contract with a king named Abimelech, whose servants had taken a well from him. The place was named Beersheba, meaning 'well of the oath' because the men agreed to have no further trouble and the well should be for Abraham's flocks and herds. I've been to Beersheba. Seven old wells are found there today."

"We should be thankful water is so plentiful. I never think about it when I turn on the faucet," admitted Bette. "I am inclined to take it for granted."

"That's the way we take many things in life," agreed Captain Lane. "I never really appreciated a good drink of cold water until one day I was traveling across the desert during the war. There was a hole in our water tank in the truck, and we didn't find out about it until we had lost all the water. We were six hours without a drink, and one soon gets thirsty in the hot desert. When we drove into camp, the pitcher of fresh, cold water they gave us tasted better than anything I ever had before or since."

"We're the same way about electric lights," Dick declared. "I know that people once used gas lights and kerosene lamps, but I can hardly imagine what it would be like. I've always been able to snap on the electric light when it was dark."

"If you had lived in Abraham's time you wouldn't have had even a kerosene lamp," Captain Lane reminded his friend. "In those days their lamps were clay dishes holding oil, with a little wick coming out of one side. You can imagine that the light was faint in the dark tents."

A brilliant sunset was coloring the sky, and the clouds were tinted a rich pink and gold. Soon the three Barretts and their friend would be home once more.

"There's one more incident in Abraham's time that you might like to think about," suggested the captain. "You remember that when Sarah died, Abraham bought the Cave of Machpelah as a family resting place."

"Abraham was buried there, too, when he died," added Dick.

10

"That's right, Dick. When you read the story in the Bible, did you notice the Oriental custom of bargaining for land? When Sarah died, Abraham went to the men of the country and told them that he was a stranger in the country and that he wanted to buy the field where the cave was located. You are a noble prince, the Hittites said to Abraham, and you should have the right to bury your dead in any cave you wish. But Abraham knew that was not the best plan. He stood up among the men and asked if they would consider selling the Cave of Machpelah to him.

"Now the man who owned the land was sitting there. His name was Ephron. With Oriental courtesy this man said he would give Abraham the land. Of course, he didn't really mean he would give him the field. He simply said that to be polite. Abraham knew this, so he bowed before the men and again said he wished to buy the field."

"What did Ephron do then? I forgot that part of the story," said Roy, his interest growing.

"Ephron declared the land was not worth very much. He said he was asking only four hundred shekels of silver for it. That is only a trifle, he told Abraham, and he added that the man should not worry about such a small amount. But Abraham knew that when Ephron stated the price he was ready to receive the money for the land. Therefore Abraham weighed out the money and gave it to Ephron for the purchase of the cave. The customs of the people in that country are the same today. They haven't changed in more than three thousand years. They have the same manners and ceremonies for purchasing land that they had in Abraham's day. I have watched them bargain for land, and the buyer and seller go through almost the same ceremony today that Abraham went through thousands of years ago."

"That helps make the Bible a living story to me," said Bette. By this time they had reached the front walk of the Lane home.

"We're home on time," said the captain, looking at his wrist watch. "And after that walk I'm really hungry. I know how Esau must have felt when he begged his brother to give him some food."

"Who was Esau?" asked Roy.

"You'll be reading about him soon in your Bible. He was so hungry he was willing to sell—; but there, I mustn't tell you the story. Read it for yourself."

"Thanks for the good time, captain," said the twins, Bette and Roy, almost in unison, following their brother, Dick, who had started on the run across the street toward home.

"I'm the one who had the fun," said the storyteller, snapping his fingers for Chips to come to the house. "Good night, and study hard for school tomorrow."

11

The ADVENTURES of TWIN BOYS

GENESIS 25:24 to 28:4

TWIN boys were born to Isaac and Rebekah, and the parents named their sons Esau and Jacob. Esau, the elder boy, was strong and bold. He liked to hike over the hills and through the valleys hunting for deer with his bow and arrows. He was a skillful hunter, and when he drew back his bow with his strong, hairy arm, the arrow went straight to its mark. Now Jacob, the younger son, was quite different from his brother. He was quiet and thoughtful, and he enjoyed watching the flocks and staying near his home.

Esau was the favorite of his father, for Isaac greatly admired his son who roamed the country as an adventurous hunter. He also enjoyed the deer meat that Esau prepared as a tasty dish. Rebekah loved Jacob more, and she spoiled him until he came to think only of himself and of having his own way.

One day Esau came home from a hunting trip. He had walked miles and miles through the wild country without seeing a deer. He was so weak and hungry he thought he was going to die. When he came near the tents of his father he saw Jacob cooking a stew of red lentils. How good the food smelled!

"Let me have a swallow of that red stuff there; for I am famishing," said Esau to his brother.

(147)

After Isaac had eaten the food, he called his son to come near, and gave him the blessing.

W. WILKE, ARTIST

Jacob should have given his hungry brother some of the food at once, but he selfishly said to Esau: "First sell me your birthright."

The birthright was the special honor given to the eldest son of the family. He took rank above his brothers and sisters, and usually his father left him the greater part of the lands, cattle, and money. The one with the birthright was specially blessed and dedicated to God, and it was his duty to care for the family when the father died.

Since Esau was easygoing and loved the carefree life of a hunter, he did not consider the birthright of much value. He said to his brother: "Here I am at the point of death; so of what use is a birthright to me?" In this way Esau promised his birthright to his brother. Then Jacob gave his hungry brother a heaping dish of bread and lentils, and Esau ate and went on his way. As Jacob saw his brother leave, he thought he had been clever to get this promise from his brother, but he had done wrong by this selfish, sinful act.

Isaac moved from place to place and finally settled at Beersheba, where his father Abraham had lived. Isaac was now an old man, and he was blind. One day he called his favorite son to his tent. "My son!" he said to him.

"Here I am," Esau replied.

"Here I am an old man, not knowing what day I may die. Get your weapons, then, your quiver and bow, and go out into the fields, and hunt some game for me. Then make me a tasty dish, such as I like, and bring it to me to eat, that I may give you my blessing before I die."

But someone else was at the door of the tent listening to

W. WILKE, ARTIST

Esau, the older son of Isaac, was easygoing and he loved the carefree life of a hunter. When he drew back his strong bow, the arrow went straight to its mark.

Isaac's words. It was his wife, Rebekah, and she wanted Jacob to have the blessing. Therefore, as Esau took his bow and arrows and started on his hunting trip, she began planning with Jacob. She told him to bring her two small goats from the flock. She cooked a dish of meat that smelled and tasted almost like the deer meat that Esau customarily prepared.

Jacob was worried. He did not like to deceive his father, and he did not want to disobey his mother. What if the plan failed? He knew his father could not see him, but he was sure Isaac would feel his arms and his neck, and Jacob was not hairy like Esau.

Rebekah had Jacob put on his best clothes, and then she took pieces of goatskin and spread them over her son's arms and neck. She put the dish of hot food in his hands and sent him to Isaac.

After returning from his successful hunt, Esau came to the tent of his father Isaac with a bowl of venison. Then the old man knew that the blessing had been stolen by Jacob.

When Jacob came near the old man, he said: "Father!" "Yes," he said. "Who are you, my son?"

Jacob said to his father: "I am Esau, your first-born; I have done as you told me; now sit up and eat once more of my game, that you may give me your blessing."

But Isaac said to his son: "However did you come to find it so quickly, my son?"

"Because the Lord your God brought it in my path," he said.

But all that Jacob said was a lie.

Then blind Isaac said: "Come up close that I may feel you, my son, to see whether you really are my son Esau or not." So Jacob went up to his father Isaac, who felt him, and said: "The voice is Jacob's voice, but the hands are those of Esau." In this way the aged father was tricked by his son Jacob.

"Are you really my son Esau?" he said.

"I am," he replied, but Jacob again told a lie to his father.

"Bring me some of your game to eat, my son, that I may give you my blessing."

The man ate the dish of tasty food and drank the wine Jacob gave him, and then he said: "Come here and kiss me, my son." Jacob went near to his father and kissed him. Isaac smelled his robes, and blessed him, saying: "Ah, my son's smell is like that of a field that the Lord has blessed.

"May God give you of the heavens' dew,
Of earth's fatness, with plenty of grain and wine!
Nations shall serve you,
And peoples bow down to you.
Be master of your brothers,
And let your mother's sons bow down to you!
Cursed be they who curse you,
And blessed be they who bless you!"

In this way Jacob received the birthright blessing from his father, and in this way he cheated Esau.

Jacob hurried from his father's tent, for he was afraid of what might happen if his brother found him there. Soon Esau came in from the hunt. He had prepared the food that Isaac loved, and he said: "Let my father sit up and eat some of his son's game, that you may give me your blessing."

"Who are you?" his father, Isaac, said to him.

"I am your son," he said, "your first-born, Esau."

The old father trembled, for he knew something was wrong. "Who was it then who got some game and brought it to me?

I ate heartily of it before you came, and blessed him, so that he is indeed blessed."

Then the strong hunter cried loud and bitterly. He knew he had been tricked by his brother, Jacob. "Bless me also, my father!" he begged.

Isaac told his son that Jacob had stolen his richest blessing, and it could not be given to another. Esau thought of his brother and said: "He stole my birthright, and now he has stolen my blessing!" Then he turned to his father: "Have you not kept a blessing for me?" he asked.

Isaac answered: "Since I have made him master over you, and have made all his brothers his slaves, and have provided grain and wine for his sustenance, what then is there that I can do for you, my son?"

For the first time in his life the carefree Esau realized that the blessing and birthright which he had counted of little value was really very important. "Have you only one blessing, my father? Bless me too, my father," he begged.

Then Isaac gave him this blessing:

> "Away from the fat of the earth shall your dwelling be,
> Away from the dew of the heavens on high.
> By your sword you shall live,
> And your brother you shall serve;
> But when you become restive,
> You shall break his yoke off your neck."

Because Jacob had cheated him, Esau hated his younger brother and said: "It will soon be time to mourn for my father, and then I will slay my brother Jacob."

Rebekah heard this threat, and she began to plan for Jacob's escape. She remembered her home in Haran where her brother Laban lived. She told her son that he must leave his father's tents and make the long journey to Haran. After a time Esau would forget the birthright, and then Jacob could come back home.

Father Isaac did not know of Esau's threat to kill Jacob, but he was anxious that his son should not marry a daughter of the people who worshiped idols. Esau had married the daughters of the people of Canaan, and it had brought sorrow to his father and mother. Isaac remembered the instruction of Abraham, and he was determined that his son should marry a daughter of his own people. Therefore he instructed Jacob to go to Haran and find a wife.

Jacob loved his home, and it was a sad day for him when he started on his lonely trip. He was worried, too, for he knew he had cheated his brother and stolen his blessing. Little did he guess how he would suffer for all the wrongs he had done to Esau.

12

JACOB FLEES *for His* LIFE

GENESIS 28:5 to 31:23

JACOB was a frightened man when he left his father's tents in Beersheba. He had never been far from home, and now he must travel more than four hundred miles on foot. For hours he walked along the road as fast as his legs would carry him; he had good reason to hurry, since his brother, Esau, might follow and take revenge on him. Jacob knew that Esau traveled over this country on some of his hunting trips. He probably imagined the hunter was hiding behind a tree or rock, ready to shoot an arrow at him.

As the lonely man hurried along the road in a country that was new and strange to him, he thought of the roving tribes of fighting men living in the hills who might attack him. One evening, as the sun was setting, he came to a place where other travelers had stopped. Jacob did not know it, but Abraham had stopped here long before when he first entered the land of Canaan.

Weary from his travel, Jacob lay down on the ground with only a round stone for a pillow. Many times during the days since he had said good-by to his father and mother, he must have thought of the wrong he had done. He was afraid when he went to sleep, but as he slept, Jacob had a wonderful dream. He saw

(155)

cob saw a flight of steps, reaching from
rth to heaven. On the steps were angels.

P. P. P. A., N. BRICE, ARTIST

a ladder, or flight of steps, bright and shining, reaching from earth to heaven. Upon the steps angels were walking up and down, and standing over him was the Lord, who said: "I am the Lord, the God of your father Abraham and of Isaac. The land on which you are lying I am going to give to you and your descendants. Your descendants shall be like the dust on the ground; you shall spread to the west, to the east, to the north, and to the south, so that all races of the earth will invoke blessings on one another through you and your descendants. I will be with you, and guard you wherever you go, and bring you back to this land; for I will never forsake you, until I have done what I have promised you."

Jacob awoke. The darkness was all about him, for the bright angels of his dream had disappeared and only the dim outline of the hills could be seen. He looked up at the stars shining in all their beauty, and he said: "The Lord must surely be in this place —and I did not know it!" As he thought of the glory of his dream, Jacob was afraid. He said: "What an awesome place this is! This can be nothing other than the house of God."

Early in the morning Jacob arose. He took the stone he had used as his pillow, and set it up for a monument. He poured some oil on it, which was the custom in making a holy place of worship, and he called the place Bethel, which means "The house of God."

As he stood there in the cool morning air he made a promise to the Lord: "If God will go with me, and watch over me on this journey that I am making, and give me food to eat and clothes to wear, so that I come home safely to my father's house, then the Lord shall be my God, and this stone which I have set

WILKE, ARTIST

Early in the morning Jacob arose and made a monument out of the stone he had used as a pillow. He poured oil on the rock and called the place Bethel, "The House of God."

up as a sacred pillar shall be God's house, and I will give to Thee a portion of everything that Thou givest me."

By this promise, Jacob said that he would give God a tenth, or tithe, of all the wealth he gained. His grandfather Abraham had given a tithe to the priest of Salem after he had rescued Lot and his family, and Isaac had told his son that it was a sacred duty to give a tenth to God.

No doubt much of the fear and loneliness left Jacob as he went on his journey from Bethel. Days passed into weeks before he arrived at Haran. As he came near the town he saw a well by the side of the road, and near the well were three flocks of sheep. Jacob stopped and asked the men who cared for the flocks where they lived. The men said they were from Haran.

"Do you know Laban, the son of Nahor?" asked Jacob.

"We do," said they.

"Is he well?" he said to them.

"He is," they said, "and here is his daughter Rachel coming with his sheep!"

He looked and, behold, a beautiful young woman was walking toward him. It was his cousin Rachel. Jacob saw that her herd of sheep were thirsty, so he rolled the stone from the top of the well and watered the sheep. Then he went to Rachel and told her that he was her cousin, the son of her father's sister, Rebekah. Jacob kissed Rachel, and he was so happy to see a relative after his long, weary journey, that tears came to his eyes.

Rachel ran to her father, Laban, and told him the news. Laban came to meet Jacob, put his arms around him, and welcomed him into his home. The man stayed with Laban and became acquainted with his sons and his two daughters, Rachel and Leah. When Jacob helped his uncle guard his flocks and herds, Laban noticed that his nephew knew how to care for the sheep and that he did his work faithfully.

After the son of Isaac and Rebekah had stayed in Haran for a month, Laban said: "Should you, just because you are a relative of mine, work for me for nothing? Let me know what your wages should be."

Jacob had fallen in love with Rachel, and hoped that someday he might marry her. In reply to Laban's question, the man said: "I will work seven years for you in return for Rachel, your younger daughter."

It was the custom of those days for a man to pay a sum of money or to give cattle or a piece of land to the father of his bride

e saw a young woman walking toward him,
ringing a flock of sheep to drink at the well.

S. A. WESTON, J. TILLACK, ARTIST

11

as a dowry. Jacob did not have rich presents to give as Abraham's servant, Eliezer, did when he took Rebekah from the family years before. Therefore the man offered to work for seven years for his bride.

Laban thought this was a good bargain, so he said: "It is better for me to give her to you than to anyone else; stay with me."

Seven years Jacob worked for his uncle, and the time passed quickly, for the man was deeply in love with Rachel. At last the day came for the marriage. A feast was prepared for the friends of the family, and everyone was merry. Jacob was a happy bridegroom. During the evening, as was the custom of the country, Laban brought the bride to Jacob. The girl had a heavy veil over her face, and no one could see her, not even her husband, until the ceremony was over.

When the time came that Jacob could see his wife, he had a terrible surprise! It was not the beautiful Rachel who was his bride, but her elder sister, Leah. Laban had deceived Jacob! Seven long years he had worked, and now he did not have for his wife the girl he loved.

Jacob went to Laban and said: "What a way for you to treat me! Did I not work with you for Rachel? Why then have you cheated me?" In his heart Jacob must have remembered how he had cheated his own brother years before. He was beginning to reap what he had sown.

Laban told Jacob it was not proper for the younger daughter to marry before her elder sister. But he agreed that if Jacob would work another seven years, he could also have Rachel for his wife. We remember that it was often the custom of those

Jacob fell in love with Rachel, the beautiful daughter of Laban who herded the flocks of sheep. The young man pledged to work seven years in order to have Rachel for his wife.

times for men to have more than one wife. Therefore, Jacob stayed and worked for Laban another seven years, and Rachel became his second wife.

After fourteen years away from his home, Jacob was anxious to return to the home of his father and mother in the land of Canaan. He said to Laban: "Let me go, that I may depart for my own home and country."

But Laban had been blessed with success while Jacob was with him, and he did not want his son-in-law to leave. So the man worked six more years, and Laban paid him with flocks of sheep and herds of cattle. Now Jacob's sheep and cattle increased rapidly, and he became wealthy. But the sons of Laban were jealous, and they complained, saying: "Jacob has taken all that our father had; it is out of what our father had that he has acquired all this wealth." This was not true, for the Lord had been good to Jacob, and had given him riches. But when Jacob saw that Laban's sons were jealous, he knew he should leave.

Memory Verses

"In the beginning God created the heaven and the earth. And the earth was without form, and void; and darkness was upon the face of the deep. And the Spirit of God moved upon the face of the waters. And God said, Let there be light: and there was light." Genesis 1:1-3.

"Thus the heavens and the earth were finished, and all the host of them. And on the seventh day God ended His work which He had made; and He rested on the seventh day from all His work which He had made." Genesis 2:1, 2.

"And the angel of the Lord called unto Abraham out of heaven the second time, and said, By Myself have I sworn, saith the Lord, for because thou hast done this thing, and hast not withheld thy son, thine only son: that in blessing I will bless thee, and in multiplying I will multiply thy seed as the stars of the heaven, and as the sand which is upon the seashore; and thy seed shall possess the gate of his enemies; and in thy seed shall all the nations of the earth be blessed; because thou hast obeyed My voice." Genesis 22:15-18.

"And Jacob vowed a vow, saying, If God will be with me, and will keep me in this way that I go, and will give me bread to eat, and raiment to put on, so that I come again to my father's house in peace; then shall the Lord be my God." Genesis 28:20, 21.

"The Lord watch between me and thee, when we are absent one from another." Genesis 31:49.

While Laban was away from home shearing his sheep, Jacob decided it was a good time to start on the journey. If he waited to tell his father-in-law good-by, the man would do everything he could to make him stay. Quickly Jacob put his two wives, his eleven sons, and his one daughter on camels, and with his flocks and herds driven by servants, the caravan started south toward Canaan, the land of his birth.

Jacob was another pioneer. Like Abraham, his grandfather, he was willing to brave danger to make his new home in the land the Lord had promised to him. But there were some dangers ahead that even Abraham did not have to face. Jacob remembered how he had cheated his brother, Esau, in stealing his birthright. Would the hunter forget the old wrong, or would he be waiting to kill Jacob?

The pioneer had something else to worry him. He was leaving Laban's home without saying good-by. His father-in-law would certainly be angry. Would he come after him? Jacob thought about these things as the caravan moved slowly along the mountain roads and in the desert country. Sometimes he wished he could hurry, so Laban would not follow him. Then again, he wished he might go more slowly, in order not to face Esau so soon.

The day came when the camels and the sheep and cattle were safely across the Euphrates River. The caravan was making good progress toward the land of Canaan. But soon Jacob heard news that troubled him. Laban was coming after him and would soon overtake his family.

All night Jacob wrestled and struggled with the strong and courageous stranger who he thought was his enemy. At daybreak the stranger gained the victory over the weary man.

(164)

13

A FIGHT in the DARK

GENESIS 31:24 to 35:28

IT WAS not until three days after Jacob left Haran with all his possessions that Laban heard the news that his son-in-law and family had gone. He was angry and started immediately in pursuit of Jacob's caravan. Over the mountain roads and across the desert Laban and his men hurried; but not until they had traveled seven days did they see the tents of Jacob pitched near Mount Gilead.

The night before Laban reached the camp, however, he was warned in a dream not to force Jacob to return to Haran. God said: "Take care to say nothing to Jacob either good or bad."

The anger of Laban was cooled by these words, and when he met Jacob he said: "What do you mean by outwitting me, and carrying off my daughters like prisoners of war? Why did you flee in secret without telling me, and rob me? I would have sent you off with mirth and songs, with tambourine and lyre. You did not even allow me to kiss my grandsons and daughters good-by! How foolishly you have acted! I had it in my power to do you harm, but the God of your father said to me the other night, 'Take care to say nothing to Jacob, either good or bad.' So now you are off, because of course you longed for your father's home!"

Jacob knew that his father-in-law would not have allowed him to leave so easily if he had told him good-by at Haran. So he answered Laban by saying: "I was afraid; for I thought that you would take your daughters from me by force."

Then Laban complained to Jacob that his family gods, or images, had been stolen. Laban lived in a land of idols, and he had heathen gods in his home. Jacob told Laban that he had not taken them, but he did not know that his wife Rachel had stolen the images and hidden them in the saddlebags of her camel.

"What is my offense; what is my misdeed, that you should have come raging after me?" asked Jacob. He reminded his father-in-law of the days and nights he had worked in winter and summer to care for his sheep. Shepherds had to watch their flocks day and night in the blazing sunshine and the frosty nights. A shepherd had to be ready to kill lions and wolves in order to protect the sheep. Jacob had done this work faithfully for Laban, yet the man had not always paid him an honest wage. Jacob reminded Laban that God had blessed him. He said: "If the God of my father, the God of Abraham and the Awe of Isaac, had not been on my side, you would now have sent me away empty-handed. God saw my suffering and the fruits of my toil."

Then Laban and Jacob made peace, and they set up a stone as a monument in that place. The other men gathered stones to make a pile of rocks about the monument. Laban and Jacob called the place Mizpah, which means "a watchtower." And Laban said: "May the Lord keep watch between you and me when we are out of one another's sight." Jacob was grateful to God for saving him from serious trouble, and he offered a sacrifice and gave thanks to the Lord.

When night came, Jacob moved his family across the river Jabbok, but he stayed behind alone to pray. It was a lonely spot in the mountains, and wild beasts waited near by.

Laban and his men ate dinner with Jacob and camped near by for the night. The next morning Laban told his daughters and his grandchildren good-by and started on his journey back to Haran.

Jacob and his family traveled on through the desert country. They were nearing Canaan, and not far to the south was Edom, the land where Esau lived. How well Jacob remembered the day over twenty years before when he had cheated his brother out of the birthright. What could he do to show Esau that he was sorry for his wrong act?

Jacob, the pioneer, decided to send his servants to Esau to tell him that he was coming home with cattle and riches. The servants were told to beg for favor and kindness from Esau. Soon the servants returned to Jacob with bad news. They told their master that Esau was coming to meet him with four hundred men. This seemed like a mighty army to helpless Jacob, and he was afraid for his family and for himself. What should he do? How could he save his wives and his children? In time of danger he turned to God and prayed:

"O Lord, God of my father Abraham and my father Isaac, who didst say to me, 'Return to your country and your kindred, and I will make you prosperous,' I do not deserve all the acts of kindness and fidelity that Thou hast shown Thy servant. . . . Save, me, I beseech Thee, from the power of my brother Esau; for I am afraid that he will come and slay me, as well as the mothers and children."

From his flocks and herds Jacob took a herd of cattle, a flock of sheep, and some camels, and sent them ahead to Esau as a present. When night came, Jacob moved his family across the River Jabbok, but he stayed behind alone to pray. It was a lonely spot in the mountains, and wild beasts were near. Suddenly a man came up to Jacob in the darkness. A strong arm was laid upon him, and fear came over him. He was sure an enemy was trying to kill him. Jacob fought for his life with all his strength. Long the struggle continued. As the day was breaking, the stranger touched Jacob's thigh and crippled him. Although he suffered from severe pain, the pioneer held on bravely while the stranger said: "Let me go; for the dawn is breaking."

But Jacob, who now realized he was wrestling with a heavenly being, said: "I will not let you go, unless you bless me."

"What is your name?" asked the stranger.

"Jacob," he replied.

"Your name shall no longer be Jacob, but Israel [wrestler with

Jacob saw his brother Esau marching toward him with his army. The valiant pioneer Jacob limped forward and bowed humbly before his brother, hoping to be forgiven.

God], because you have wrestled with God and man, and have been the victor."

And the stranger from heaven blessed Jacob, and Jacob called the place Peniel, which means "face of God," for he said: "I have seen God face to face, and yet my life has been spared." Now there was courage in Jacob's heart, for he knew that the Lord had been with him in time of trouble, and had given him a special blessing.

When the sun rose that morning, Jacob made his way across the river to the camp where his wives and children were waiting for him. He limped as he walked, for he had been crippled in wrestling with the heavenly One.

Soon Jacob saw his brother marching toward him with his army of four hundred men. The valiant pioneer arranged his

family in groups to protect them, and then he went forward to
meet Esau, limping painfully as he walked. The women and
children stood watching. Would the brothers fight? Would
Esau try to kill Jacob? Jacob bowed before his brother seven
times, an honor due to a chief of the country. Esau ran to meet
Jacob and threw his arms around him. The old hatred was forgotten, and the brothers loved each other.

"What relation are these to you?" asked Esau, pointing to the
women and children.

"The children whom God has graciously bestowed on your
servant," Jacob replied, as he introduced Esau to his family.
Esau asked why the cattle, sheep, and camels had been sent to
him, and Jacob explained that they were a present. At first the
man from Edom refused to accept them. "I have plenty, my
brother," said Esau; "keep what you have." But with much urg-
ing Esau finally agreed to keep the cattle, sheep, and camels
which his brother had given him.

After a short visit the brothers parted in peace. Esau returned
to his home in the desert country of Edom, and his brother led
his caravan across the Jordan River to the town of Shechem.
Now Jacob was anxious for his family to worship the true God
with all their hearts. So he took the idols that he found his wives
had carried with them from Haran, and he buried them. Later
he moved his family to Bethel, where he built an altar and worshiped. He gave thanks for God's protection and blessing to him
during the long years since that lonely night when he had slept
there as a weary man running away from trouble. He remembered his dream of angels on the stairway leading from earth to
heaven.

Jacob was anxious to see his aged father, Isaac. He journeyed on with his family, his flocks, and his herds. But before he reached his father's tents at Hebron, Rachel, his favorite wife, died. She left her husband a baby son who was named Benjamin. Rachel was buried at Bethlehem, and Jacob erected a monument at her grave.

Jacob finally arrived at Hebron. Isaac, his father, was feeble, and he did not live long after Jacob returned. He was one hundred eighty years of age when he died, and Jacob and Esau laid him to rest in the Cave of Machpelah.

When Rachel died, Jacob buried the body of his wife at Bethlethem. Today a costly shrine has been erected where Rachel's tomb is traditionally said to have been located.

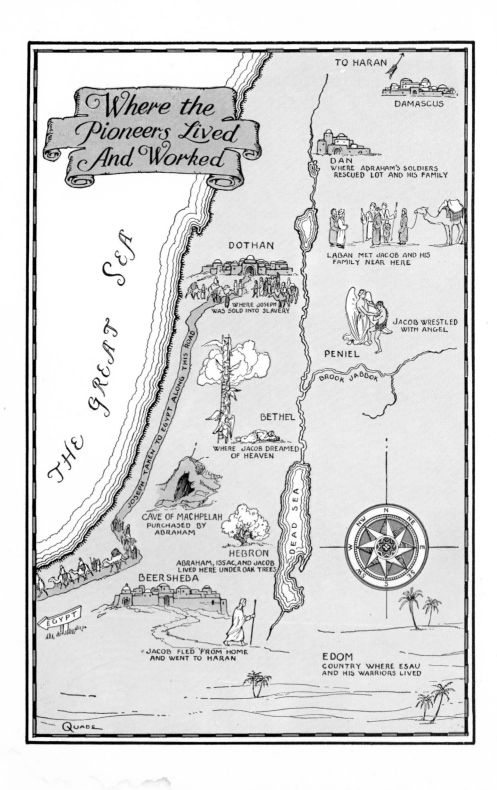

Captain Tim's Bible Quiz

"Ask us some more Bible questions," said Bette and Roy Barrett to Captain Tim, after they had finished reading the story of the Tower of Babel, and the adventures of Abraham, Isaac, and Jacob.

"All right," said Captain Tim. "I'll ask you some questions on what you have read in Genesis between chapters 10 and 34."

See if you can answer these Bible questions as well as the Barretts did. The answers are on page 251.

1. What mighty hunter lived on the earth soon after the Flood?
2. Who was the mother of Isaac?
3. Where did men build a tower which they planned would reach to heaven?
4. Near what cities did Lot pitch his tent after he left Abram?
5. Who was the mother of Ishmael?
6. What did Abraham offer on the altar in place of his son Isaac?
7. How long did Jacob work for his first wife?
8. Who had a stone for his pillow when he slept in the open country at night?
9. Name the two brothers who were twins.
10. How many persons were saved when Sodom was destroyed?
11. How did God stop the work on the great tower that men were building?
12. Who wrestled with an angel at night?
13. Where did Abraham send his servant to find a wife for Isaac?
14. Who became a pillar of salt?
15. How many men did Esau have with him when he met Jacob coming back to Canaan?
16. What was the new name given to Jacob?
17. Who saw a camel caravan and knew his bride was coming?
18. Where did Abram go when there was a famine in Canaan?
19. Who was kidnaped by enemy kings?
20. Who came to warn Lot to leave Sodom?

FROM DAN *to* BEERSHEBA

"W HAT'S going on upstairs?" asked Bette Barrett, as a dull thud echoed through the hall.

"I don't know, dear," replied her mother. "Dick went to the attic more than an hour ago. He said he wanted to find his tennis racket. Perhaps you should go see what he's doing."

Mrs. Barrett and Bette were in the sewing room—a cozy corner of the house, particularly today, when the autumn wind and rain made the out-of-doors dreary. Mrs. Barrett was doing the family mending—a job she saved for rainy days, and Bette was curled up in a big chair reading to her mother.

Another thud shook the walls, and Bette jumped from the chair and ran into the hall. "Dick will tear the house down if he isn't careful," she called back to her mother as she went up the stairs two steps at a time.

At the door of the attic storeroom the girl stopped and surveyed the scene. "What are you doing, Dick?"

"How did you know I was here?" asked the boy innocently, without answering Bette's question.

"We couldn't miss you, that's certain. The banging on the ceiling almost shook the house."

"I guess I tipped over a couple of those," the boy admitted,

(174)

"Let's look at this together," said the captain. "I've always been interested in maps

W. WILKE, ART

pointing to the large cartons overturned on the floor. "But nothing was hurt."

"What are you doing with that stack of books, Dick?"

"I was moving them to get to the box that had my tennis racket, when they spilled. Don't scold me; I know it's a mess!"

Books, large and small, were scattered over the floor; they had spread in all directions as they fell. Bette looked at them and then at her touseled-haired brother and decided it was time to help him. She began putting books into the half-empty box.

"Don't worry about me or the books, Bette. I'll get them put away." Dick was helping his sister pick up the volumes as he made his apology.

"I haven't anything to do for a while, and you certainly need help. Look, Dick, here is a scrapbook I made three years ago. It took hours of work, and was I happy when it was finished! What is the big book you have there?"

Dick looked at the cover carefully and then opened the book. "It's an atlas of Bible lands," he said. "It has maps of the towns and countries mentioned in the Old and the New Testament, according to the title page."

"Let me look at it, too," requested Bette. "Since reading many of the Bible stories, I've wanted to know more about the land of Palestine." The girl turned the pages until she came to a colored map. "Here is a map of the travels of Abraham, Isaac, and Jacob," she said.

"Let's see what we can find on it," Dick suggested.

"The light isn't good here. Why don't we put things away and go downstairs where we can have light and be comfortable while we look at it?"

"We might go over to Captain Tim's study," Dick replied, as he finished stacking books. "He'd like to see these maps, too."

"All right." Bette looked out the small window as she spoke. "Here comes Roy from the library. He doesn't seem to mind the rain at all."

"Let's go, then," said Dick, snapping the light switch and following his sister down the stairway. Roy was entering the sewing room as Dick and Bette arrived to announce their plan. Mrs. Barrett was willing for the children to go, and Roy was anxious to join his brother and sister on their proposed visit to Captain Lane's study.

"What do you have tucked under your arm, Dick?" were Captain Lane's first words as he greeted the Barrett trio at his front door.

"We have something we think you'd like to see," said Bette, her eyes sparkling.

After the trio had followed the captain into his book-lined study, Dick opened the atlas and laid it flat on the desk.

"This looks like a good Bible atlas," Captain Lane said. "Where did you get it?"

"I ran across it in our attic this afternoon," Dick explained. "Bette and I started to look at it, but we decided we would like to share it with you."

"Here is the map we were especially interested in, Captain Tim." Bette turned to the page on which the travels of Abraham, Isaac, and Jacob were depicted.

"Bring up some chairs, Roy, and let's look at this together," said the man. "I've always been interested in maps."

"This is ancient Babylon in the valley of the Tigris and Euphrates Rivers. This is where the Tower of Babel is said to have been built. Ur, the birthplace of Abraham, is here near the Persian Gulf." The captain was using his pencil to point out familiar names on the map.

"Look at this crescent-shaped chain of cities. They reach from Babylon up north to Haran and then south and west through Palestine to Egypt. This has been called 'the Fertile Crescent,' for it was land that was well-watered. The crops could grow and the cattle and sheep could have good pasture. Abraham left his home in Ur and probably journeyed along the Euphrates River until he came to Haran. After his father died, he left the land of Mesopotamia and traveled to Palestine."

"Here are some of the places where Abraham lived in Canaan," said Roy, looking ahead of the captain's pencil.

A modern girl of Palestine carries a pitcher of water on her head in the same way Rebekah did more than three thousand years ago.

THREE LIONS

"You're always one jump ahead of me, Roy," said the man with a laugh. "One of the first stops that Abraham made in the land that God promised him was near Shechem. It is about thirty miles north of Jerusalem. You can see it here on the map."

"Did you ever visit that part of Palestine, Captain Tim?" asked Bette.

"Yes, I made a trip south from Damascus during the first World War. We stopped at the place where Shechem used to be. The town has another name today. Before we arrived there we drove through a mountain pass where we could look down on the green valley. To the north is Mount Ebal and on the south, Mount Gerizim. Shechem was once a strong city of defense because it guarded this pass. The walls of the old fort have been found by archaeologists."

"It was near Bethel that Abraham pitched his tents after he moved on from Shechem," Dick said, as he pointed to the dot on the map. "I remember he built an altar there."

"Bethel was probably a town with strong walls around it when Abraham visited it."

"Did most of the people live in walled cities?" asked Roy.

"It seems that in ancient times the farmers lived in the towns, but they went out to their fields every day to work. It was necessary to live in the walled cities for protection from enemies," Captain Lane explained.

"I suppose it was a common thing for chiefs to attack cities and carry away prisoners, as they did Lot and his family."

"Yes, it must have been, Roy; but Abraham, Isaac, and Jacob were certainly protected by God, for we do not hear of their being attacked."

"Since there was constant danger, I imagine Abraham was wise to have his servants trained to fight," suggested Bette.

"It was at the gates of these walled cities that many interesting business transactions took place," went on Captain Lane. "The judges and other officials often sat at the gate. Here they could see everyone who came in and went out of the city. Business was transacted and property bought and sold. You remember that Abraham purchased the Cave of Machpelah from the children of Heth at the gate of the town. If you wanted to write to a friend or relative, you could go to men who had little tables

Traveling northward from Jerusalem, we would find the well of Joseph on the plains of Dothan. Tradition declares that this is the pit in which Joseph was placed by his brothers.

by the wall, and they would write the letter for you. They were the secretaries of those days."

"That helps one understand why Lot was sitting at the gate of the city of Sodom when the angels arrived," Roy declared.

"Yes, he must have been a prominent man and was there on business. He knew the city was very wicked, too, and when strangers came, he could invite them to his home and protect them from harm," the man continued.

"I imagine Abraham enjoyed living on the plains of Mamre more than any other place he lived," Bette spoke up.

"Why do you think so?" asked her twin brother.

"Well, Roy, for one reason, he went back there more than once after he lived in other places. I'm sure the shady oak trees were an ideal spot if one lived in tents. Then, too, his son Isaac was born there," the girl explained.

"Don't forget that the Cave of Machpelah was near Mamre, and Abraham bought it for a tomb when Sarah died," Dick added, coming to the aid of his sister.

"Mamre was about halfway between Jerusalem and Beersheba," said the captain. "Both Abraham and Isaac had some exciting adventures at Beersheba."

"What do people mean when they say, 'From Dan to Beersheba'?" asked Roy, rising from his chair and going to stand before the warm glow of the fire in the fireplace.

"Put some wood on the fire, Roy, if you will," suggested the man. "Then come here and look at the map and you will see. Beersheba is at the southern boundary of the land of Palestine. Where is Dan?"

"I thought that Dan was a person—one of the sons of Jacob," spoke up Bette quickly.

"Well, that's true. But Dan is also the name of a town at the northern edge of Palestine. So when you say, 'From Dan to Beersheba,' it means covering all the territory, as we say, 'From Maine to California.'"

"What does Beersheba mean?"

"Let me think!" Captain Lane rubbed his chin as he tried to remember. "I fear I've forgotten. It has something to do with a well. Look it up, Dick. There's a Bible on the corner of the table. You'll find the story in Genesis."

"Which chapter?" asked the searcher.

"I'm not certain. But look in the back of the Bible under the index of proper names. Do you find that?"

"Index of proper names. Yes, here it is right after the Revelation in this Bible," Dick replied. "Now, then, to find Beersheba. The reference is to Genesis 21. But the meaning of the name is given, too. 'Beersheba—well of the oath,' it says."

"Good enough. Perhaps that will help you find names in the Bible easier. Don't forget to look in the index of proper names. Beersheba was a town on the edge of the desert. Water was precious, and it was necessary for Abraham and Isaac to dig wells to get water for their flocks and herds. A man named Abimelech disputed their right to the wells; but it was all settled peaceably. When I visited Beersheba, a shepherd took me to the places of interest. I saw several of the wells which are supposed to have been there since the days of Isaac. You can see the grooves in the stones that form the wall of the wells. They

The Dead Sea is about thirteen hundred feet below normal sea level, and is the lowest body of water on the earth. The sea is extremely salty, and the country around is bare.

KEYSTONE

are grooves worn in the rock by the leather straps used by the women to pull buckets of water from the well."

"Do men know anything about the cities of Sodom and Gomorrah, Captain Tim?" queried Bette. "I see the names on the map in curves. What does that mean?"

"Yes, there they are," the captain said, pointing out the location to the boys. "It is thought that the cities were located near the southeast corner of the Dead Sea. This sea, as you know, is down in a deep valley. In fact, it is about thirteen hundred feet below the level of the Mediterranean, and is the lowest body of water on the earth's surface. The river Jordan, fed by cold mountain streams and melting snow, flows south and empties into the Dead Sea. The sea is extremely salty, and the country around it is bleak and bare."

"But Sodom and Gomorrah were once in a beautiful valley, the Bible says," Dick declared.

"Yes, but remember they were destroyed. It is believed the south end of the Dead Sea now covers the place where the cities were. Asphalt and oil have been discovered in that region. We know a great catastrophe occurred there for the country around the sea shows the results of fire and explosion. The Bible story seems to be unquestioned. No doubt this is the graveyard of those two wicked cities." As Captain Lane finished his story, he arose and went over to a bookcase. Opening one of the doors, he brought out a small bottle of water. "This is a sample of the water from the Dead Sea. It contains five times as much salt as ocean water," he explained. "I filled the bottle when I made my second trip there."

"I read recently, Captain Tim, about science using the water of the Dead Sea to make chemical compounds, dyes, and in making antiknock gasoline," Roy announced.

"Yes, the last time I was at the Dead Sea they were beginning work," Captain Lane stated.

"Tell us more about the land of Palestine. I'd surely like to go there sometime," Bette said wistfully.

"Yes, is it anything like America?" asked Dick.

"Not in size, anyway," replied Captain Lane. "Most of the thrilling events of the Old Testament happened in a land no larger than the State of Connecticut. You see, the entire country is only about one hundred fifty miles long from Dan to Beersheba. It is even narrower. Up at the northern end it is only about thirty miles wide, while down at the south it is sixty-four miles from Gaza to the Dead Sea."

"Think how many wonderful things happened in such a small country!" exclaimed the girl.

"The country has a great deal of variety, though. You can go to snow-capped mountains, such as Mount Hermon, 9,700 feet above sea level; or you can drop down to the Dead Sea, 1,292 feet below sea level. It is cool on the Mediterranean Sea, but intensely hot in the desert. There are valleys and rolling hills, rugged barren canyons and wooded slopes. So you can find almost anything you like for climate and scenery in the land of Palestine."

"This means a lot to me," Dick was saying as he looked at the clock over the fireplace. "I have a theme to write on Egypt, and now I have a link between Palestine and the land of the Nile River. I'll start work on it tonight if I have time."

Captain Lane smiled. "We are interested in Egypt, too. So

when you have the theme written, let's hear it, Dick. We are going to visit Egypt soon with our Bible heroes."

"Is that so, Captain Tim? All right, then, this will be doubly interesting to me. I'll see what I can find out about Egypt. With your help I should get an A grade."

"We're glad to go places with you, captain, even when it's only in imagination," said Roy, as he picked up his umbrella from the stand in the hall.

"We can get home in a hurry after this kind of trip. Let's go!" Dick called as he turned up his coat collar and braved the raindrops.

"Good night," called the man to his three friends as they disappeared in the gray twilight and misty rain.

14

JOSEPH the DREAMER

GENESIS 37; 38

JACOB made his home at Hebron, pitching his tents in the shade of the spreading oak trees. Since he was growing old he spent much of his time during the day at the door of his tent, resting on rugs and cushions. He was the chief of his people, and his twelve sons were in charge of the sheep and cattle that grazed in the meadows and on the hillsides. Jacob's sons were named Reuben, Simeon, Levi, Judah, Dan, Naphtali, Gad, Asher, Issachar, Zebulun, Joseph, and Benjamin. Joseph and Benjamin were the sons of Rachel, and the youngest boys in the family. Therefore they were Jacob's favorites. Joseph was honest and stronghearted, a youth who could be depended on to do his work well. His father loved to walk with him through the fields, telling him about God and how the world was created. Joseph enjoyed playing with his younger brother, Benjamin. The boys could help, as shepherds' sons often did, by filling snake holes so the sheep would not step in them and break a leg. And sometimes they might draw water from the well for the cattle.

Jacob's ten older sons were not good men. They were selfish and quarrelsome, and often they told lies and deceived their father. When Joseph saw his brothers doing wrong it troubled

(187)

him, and he tried to get them to do right; but they only hated him for his words of reproof.

To show Joseph how much he loved him, his father gave him a beautiful robe of fine cloth. It was a coat of many bright colors, which any boy would be proud to own. Most of the shepherd boys wore only a plain shirt and a leather girdle. Therefore, it was a special honor for Joseph to put on this bright coat and parade before his brothers. But it was not wise for Jacob to show his love for one son above another; and it was not the right thing for Joseph to show off in front of his brothers. When the ten brothers saw him in the beautiful coat they scowled, and in their hearts they hated him as Cain once hated Abel.

At the time of harvest Joseph helped cut the grain and bind it in sheaves. One night when he was seventeen years old he had a dream, and the next morning he told it to his brothers. He said: "Listen to this dream that I have had. While we were binding sheaves in the field, my sheaf rose up and remained standing, while your sheaves gathered round it, and made obeisance to my sheaf!"

This dream made his brothers frown, and they said scornfully: "Are you indeed to be king over us; would you actually rule us?"

A little later Joseph had a second dream, and again he told it to his brothers. He told them that in his dream he saw the bright sun, the silver moon, and eleven stars, shining in the heavens. As he watched, he said, he saw in his dream the sun, moon, and stars bow before him.

His brothers were angry, and they hated him more and more because of his dreams and because he was proud of his beautiful coat and wore it so that they had to look at it. When Jacob heard of his son's dreams, he wondered if God was telling the family that Joseph would someday become a great man.

During the hot summer days the grass dried up in the meadows, and the ten brothers drove the flocks of sheep to the north where there was better pasture. After they had been gone for some time, Jacob was anxious to know how they were getting along. He called Joseph to his tent and told him he wanted to hear from his ten sons.

"Are not your brothers pasturing the flocks at Shechem? Come, let me send you to them," said the father to Joseph.

"I am ready," he replied.

Jacob instructed the youth, saying: "Go and see how your brothers are, and the flocks; and bring me back word."

The youth was excited with the thought of adventure. He had never been far from home, and now he was going on a journey of about fifty miles. This was a long distance in those days, for one either walked or rode on a slow-moving donkey. With a joyful heart Joseph left his father's tents and made his way over the hills and through the valleys until he came to Shechem. When he arrived at the town he could not find his brothers. A man found Joseph searching here and there, and said to him: "What are you looking for?"

"I am looking for my brothers," he said; "do tell me where they are pasturing the flocks."

The man said: "They have moved from here; for I heard them say, 'Let us go to Dothan.'"

Joseph took the road to Dothan and walked the fifteen miles farther. From a hilltop he saw his brothers with their flocks of sheep. Although he had trudged many miles he ran down the slope waving and shouting to them.

When the brothers saw Joseph coming across the fields, they began to talk about him. They made fun of his dreams and spoke scornfully of his beautiful coat. Some of the brothers who hated Joseph the most suggested that they should kill him.

"There comes the dreamer yonder!" they said to one another. "Come now, let us kill him, and throw him into one of the pits. We can say that a wild beast devoured him. Then we shall see what his dreams will come to."

Reuben, the eldest, was more kindhearted than the other brothers. He said: "Do not shed any blood; throw him into the pit here in the wilderness, but do not lay hands on him."

While the brothers were arguing, Joseph came running up. The men did not greet him with words of welcome. Instead,

The brothers grabbed Joseph, threw him on the ground, and tore his beautiful coat. The youth begged for mercy, but the cruel men picked him up and threw him into a pit.

W. WILKE, ARTIST

When the caravan came near, the brothers hailed the leader. They bargained with the crafty merchant, and agreed to sell young Joseph for twenty pieces of silver.

they grabbed him roughly, threw him on the ground, and tore his coat of many colors. The youth cried and begged for mercy, but his cruel brothers would not listen. They picked him up and threw him into a dark pit, which, fortunately, did not have any water in it.

Then the hardhearted men sat down to eat their dinner. Do you think you could enjoy your food if you had treated your brother cruelly? Reuben did not want to hear Joseph's cries, so he left his brothers. He intended to come back later and rescue the youth from the pit. But while he was gone, a caravan of Ishmaelite traders came along the road, and the brothers plotted a terrible crime.

13

Jacob, the aged pioneer, who dearly loved Joseph, looked at the bloodstained coat and cried: "It is my son's cloak!" The wicked sons stood silent and ashamed before him.

When Judah saw the camels loaded with precious goods, he said: "What is the good of killing our brother and covering up his blood? Come, let us sell him to the Ishmaelites, and not lay hands on him."

The caravan came near, and the brothers hailed the leader. They offered to sell Joseph to him as a slave. The crafty merchant looked at the strong youth and offered to buy him for twenty pieces of silver. The brothers agreed, and Joseph was bound with ropes and carried away by the traders. As the caravan of camels disappeared over the hills, there must have been guilty looks on the faces of the brothers. They had sold their younger brother to be a slave, a fate often worse than death itself.

Later, Reuben returned to help Joseph out of the deep pit.

But when he called, there was no answer. Where was Joseph!

Greatly worried at the disappearance of the youth, Reuben ran to his brothers, saying: "The boy is gone! And I, how can I go home?"

The brothers had to explain what had happened. Now they were afraid, for how could they go home and face their father? What would they say had happened to Joseph? In an attempt to deceive Jacob they took the beautiful coat and dipped it in the blood of a goat. Then they started toward home, dreading the time when they would have to face their father. As they came near their father's tents, he was waiting for them. He asked them if they had seen Joseph. Giving the bloodstained coat to Jacob, they said: "We found this; see whether it is your son's cloak or not." Thus they tried to cover up their crime with a lie.

The aged pioneer, who dearly loved Joseph, looked at the coat and touched it with trembling hands. Then he cried out: "It is my son's cloak! Some wild beast has devoured him; Joseph must be torn to pieces."

As was the custom of the country when a person was in sorrow, Jacob tore his clothing and put on a rough cloth called "sackcloth." For days he sat in his tent mourning for his lost son. Day after day the ten brothers heard the cries of their father, and they knew it was their wicked deed that broke his heart. They spoke to him, but Jacob would not be comforted.

Probably the brothers said to one another: "Well, we have gotten rid of Joseph. We can forget about him now! Nothing will come of his dreams, that's certain."

But God was watching over Joseph, and, as the years went by, the brothers would find they could never forget him!

15

A SLAVE *in* PRISON

GENESIS 39; 40

JOSEPH trudged along the dusty road with the camel caravan of the Ishmaelites. Tears were in his eyes as he thought of his home at Hebron. He looked at the hills to the east and knew that his father's tents were near, for the caravan journeyed south on a road that was only a few miles from his home. He had been loved and honored all his life, but now he was a slave. He had learned to have faith in God, and in this hour of trouble he prayed for help. He determined to be strong and do what was right, for his father had always trusted him.

The caravan took the road along the sea, and after a time Joseph found that the traders were heading for Egypt. This news made him sick at heart, for Egypt was a strange, foreign land, and he knew his chances of ever returning home were growing less with every mile he traveled. The day came when the camel train arrived at the frontier wall where there was a strong fort. The Egyptian guards opened and inspected all the bundles the camels carried. When everything was checked, the caravan moved on into the land of the Nile River.

Egypt was a strange sight to Joseph. He saw temples, great pyramids, horses and chariots, and swift boats sailing on the

(195)

The merchant who bought young Joseph took him as a slave into the land of Egypt.

broad river. At the capital city the traders sold Joseph to Potiphar, the captain of the king's guard. Even as a slave, Joseph decided that he would work faithfully and do his best to please his master.

The young man learned to speak the language of Egypt, and he did his work so well that Potiphar gave him charge over his house and over all his property. God was with Joseph, and the king's officer was pleased to find a slave who could be trusted.

Joseph held his position in Potiphar's house for ten years, when a severe test came to him. Potiphar's wife, a wicked woman, tried to get Joseph to do wrong. But the young man loved God and remained true and upright. Then the woman was angry, and she told lies about him to her husband. Potiphar was angry and commanded that Joseph be cast into prison.

Days and weeks passed, and no one came to help the young man who lay chained in the dark prison. He had no friends or relatives in the country to help him. But in spite of this unfair punishment, Joseph determined to obey his God and do right. After a time the jailer noticed Joseph and gave him work to do. He was faithful and honest in all that he did, and the jailer found that he could trust him with many prison duties.

One day there was great excitement at the prison. Two notable officers of the palace were imprisoned by order of the Egyptian king, who was called Pharaoh. The two officers were the king's butler and baker. The butler prepared all the wine for the king, and the baker made all his bread and cakes. It seems that Pharaoh had become angry with these men and had sent them to prison.

Joseph was given the task of caring for these prisoners. One morning when he came to visit the butler and the baker in their cell he saw that they were worried. "Why do you look so gloomy today?" he asked.

"We have had dreams," they replied, "and there is no one to interpret them."

Joseph said to them: "Does not dream interpretation belong to God? Pray recount them to me."

So the butler of Pharaoh told Joseph his dream. "In my dream," he said, "there was a vine in front of me, and on the vine were three branches. As soon as it budded, its blossoms shot up, its clusters ripened into grapes. With Pharaoh's cup in my hand, I took the grapes, and squeezing them into Pharaoh's cup, I placed the cup in Pharaoh's hand."

Joseph listened closely to the butler's words. He remembered the dreams he had as a youth at home. God was with Joseph and made the meaning of this dream clear to him. He said to the butler: "This is its interpretation: the three branches represent three days; within three days Pharaoh shall summon you, and restore you to your position, so that you shall place Pharaoh's cup in his hand as you used to do when you were his butler."

Then the baker was anxious to tell his dream to Joseph, for he had heard the good words that were spoken to the butler. He said to Joseph: "I too had a dream; in mine there were three openwork baskets on my head, and in the top basket was some of every kind of baked food for Pharaoh, but the birds were eating it out of the basket on my head."

When Joseph heard the dream, he was sad; but he courageously told the baker the truth, although he knew it would bring him great sorrow. Joseph said: "This is its interpretation: the three baskets represent three days; within three days Pharoah shall summon you, and hang you on a tree, and the birds shall eat the flesh off you."

In three days Pharoah's birthday was celebrated with a great feast. The king sent for the butler and the baker and considered their cases. He restored the butler to his royal position, but the baker was hanged. Thus Joseph's words proved true, for God was with him.

Before the butler left the prison, Joseph asked a favor of him. This man was in the royal palace, and he might be able to tell Pharoah about any prisoner who should be set free. "So, if you will be good enough to keep me in mind when prosperity comes to you," said Joseph, "do me the kindness of mentioning me to Pharoah, and so liberate me from this house; for I was really

Joseph told the meaning of the dreams to the king's butler and baker. The butler was happy when he heard the interpretation, but the baker cried when he realized his doom.

W. WILKE, ARTIST

kidnaped from the land of the Hebrews, and further, I have done nothing here that I should be put into a dungeon."

As Joseph watched the butler go back to the palace, he hoped that the man would remember him. But days, weeks, and months dragged by, and nothing happened. The butler had forgotten his promise made after Joseph's kindness. Behind the prison bars an innocent man still wondered when his prayers would be answered. Would he ever be set free from this Egyptian prison? Here was a servant of the king of Egypt who might be able to speak a good word in his behalf. Joseph was homesick for his father's house. He longed to be free to return to the land of Canaan. As Joseph thought of his home, he prayed that God might use the butler to help him.

What a lesson in remembering the good deed that a friend does for us! Too often we take little kindnesses for granted, and we forget to help others in their hour of need. The butler forgot his promise, and because of his neglect Joseph stayed for weeks and months in prison.

16

FROM PRISON *to* PALACE

GENESIS 41

IN THE palace of Pharaoh all was excitement and confusion. On this particular morning the courtiers were alarmed, and the servants talked in whispers behind closed doors. Pharaoh was angry; he was shouting commands and making fearful threats.

Now the butler heard what had happened. One of the servants told him that Pharaoh was troubled because of two strange dreams which seemed to have a special message for him and for his country. He was worried, for he could not understand the meaning of the dreams.

While the butler worked in the royal palace he saw the wise men of the nation hurrying to and fro. Pharaoh had called them to tell him the meaning of his dreams. He had told them the dreams, and they had searched diligently in books of magic for an answer; but they could find nothing to help the king. Soon there was an angry shout, and the guards led the wise men out of the court. The king had commanded the men to leave because they had failed to help him.

Again the servants talked together and the courtiers met in the palace. What could be done for their noble ruler? Suddenly the butler remembered his dream in prison and how Joseph had

(201)

seph was brought to the king's palace
d stood before the throne of Pharaoh.

WILKE, ARTIST

Royal messengers ran to the prison and the jailer released Joseph. Then he was hurried through the city streets to the palace. The son of Jacob would now stand before Pharaoh.

given him its true meaning. Yes, what Joseph had said had come to pass; but the butler had forgotten his friend for two long years! Quickly the butler went to Pharaoh with a cup of wine. He told his ruler about Joseph and begged him to send for the prisoner.

Eager to find anyone who could help him, Pharaoh acted at once. To call on a foreigner in prison to tell him the meaning of the dream was an unheard-of thing; but the king was anxious to find anyone who could tell him the truth. Royal messengers ran to the prison and ordered the jailer to release Joseph so that he could go to the king's palace. The son of Jacob was thrilled by the news! Perhaps there was hope of release. Joseph was quickly prepared for this strange adventure. His face and head were shaved and he was dressed in spotless linen garments, as was the custom of the Egyptians.

Then the king's guards placed Joseph in a chariot, and the horses set off at a gallop. Upon arriving at the palace, he was led into the court where Pharaoh sat upon a golden throne. Joseph, who was now thirty years old, looked upon the ruler with wonder. The king of Egypt wore a high crown on which was fastened a gold snake. On his hand was a ring, a sign of royal power. At the side of the magnificent throne stood the courtiers, officers, and a royal guard of soldiers. It was a breath-taking moment for Joseph, but he stood fearlessly awaiting the king's words.

"I have had a dream," Pharaoh said to Joseph, "but there is no one to interpret it. However, I have heard it said of you that you know how to interpret dreams."

"Apart from God can Pharaoh be given a favorable response?" Joseph answered Pharaoh, thus admitting he did not have wisdom in himself to interpret the dreams.

Then the ruler told Joseph what he had dreamed. He said: "I dreamed that I was standing on the bank of the Nile, when seven fat and beautiful cows came up out of the Nile, and browsed in the sedge. After them came up seven other cows, thin and very ugly and lean—I have never seen such poor cows in all the land of Egypt. Then the lean, ugly cows ate up the first seven fat cows; they passed right into them, but no one would have known that they had done so—they looked just as bad as before. Then I awoke.

"In another dream I saw seven ears of grain growing on a single stalk, full and plump, and after them there sprouted seven other ears, withered, thin, and blasted by the east wind. Then the thin ears swallowed up the seven plump ears." When he had spoken these words, Pharaoh waited eagerly for a reply.

Joseph, pale from his long imprisonment, looked at the monarch on his throne. He told Pharaoh that his two dreams had the same meaning. God was showing Pharaoh what was about to happen to his country. The seven fat cows and the seven plump ears of grain represented the next seven years, when Egypt would have good crops and rich harvests. But after that there would come seven terrible years of famine, represented by the poor cows and the lean ears of grain.

Pharaoh listened to every word Joseph spoke. He saw in this prisoner a man of strength and ability, a man who had faith in God. After Joseph had revealed the meaning of the dreams, he continued speaking. He said: "Now, then, let Pharaoh find a shrewd and prudent man, and put him in control of the land of Egypt. Let Pharaoh proceed to appoint officials over the land to forearm the land of Egypt during the seven years of plenty; let them collect all the food of these good years that are coming, and under the authority of Pharaoh store up grain for food in the cities, and hold it there. The food shall serve as a reserve for the land against the seven years of famine that are to befall the land of Egypt, so that the land may not perish from the famine."

When he had said this he bowed and stood in his place. Pharaoh sat in thought for a moment and then said to his courtiers: "Can we find a man with the spirit of God in him like this one?" Then, turning to Joseph, he said: "I hereby put you in charge of the whole land of Egypt."

Joseph must have felt as if he were in a dream. Only a few

Memory Verses

"And he said unto him, What is thy name? And he said, Jacob. And he said, Thy name shall be called no more Jacob, but Israel: for as a prince hast thou power with God and with men, and hast prevailed." Genesis 32:27, 28.

"And the Lord was with Joseph, and he was a prosperous man; and he was in the house of his master the Egyptian. And his master saw that the Lord was with him, and that the Lord made all that he did to prosper in his hand." Genesis 39:2, 3.

"And Joseph answered Pharaoh, saying, It is not in me: God shall give Pharaoh an answer of peace." Genesis 41:16.

"And Joseph said unto his brethren, I am Joseph; doth my father yet live? And his brethren could not answer him; for they were troubled at his presence. And Joseph said unto his brethren, Come near to me, I pray you. And they came near. And he said, I am Joseph your brother, whom ye sold into Egypt. Now therefore be not grieved, nor angry with yourselves, that ye sold me hither: for God did send me before you to preserve life." Genesis 45:3-5.

"And Jacob said unto Pharaoh, The days of the years of my pilgrimage are an hundred and thirty years: few and evil have the days of the years of my life been, and have not attained unto the days of the years of the life of my fathers in the days of their pilgrimage." Genesis 47:9.

"And Israel said unto Joseph, Behold, I die: but God shall be with you, and bring you again unto the land of your fathers." Genesis 48:21.

The Nile River was the life line of Egypt, for each year melting snows in the mountains caused the river to flood the fields. Then the Egyptians could look for a rich harvest.

hours before he had been in the dark dungeon; but now he was a royal official next to Pharaoh himself! The king took the royal ring from his finger and put it upon the hand of Joseph. He commanded that the newly appointed official be dressed in beautiful robes from the king's wardrobe, and that a golden chain be put around his neck.

A royal chariot pulled by stately horses was presented to Joseph, and when he, as the new governor of the land, rode through the streets or along the country roads, servants ran before him shouting for the people to bow in homage to him.

Soon Joseph made a trip through all the land of Egypt. He

saw how the Nile River rose and flooded the fields. He watched the Egyptians plowing, planting the grain, and preparing for the harvest. During the next seven years the land was filled with plenty. Great storehouses were built, and so much grain was stored away that Joseph could not keep a complete account of it.

Joseph married an Egyptian maiden named Asenath, and they had two sons. Their first boy was called Manasseh, meaning "forgetfulness," because Joseph said God had helped him forget his imprisonment and trouble. Their second son was named Ephraim, meaning "fruitfulness," because God had made Joseph to prosper in Egypt.

When the seven years of abundant crops had passed, Joseph awaited the next year. Would it be a time of famine as he had told Pharaoh? At the time of year when the Nile River usually flooded the country, the water grew shallow instead. The land was not watered, and the grain withered and died in the fields. The grass grew brown and dried up so that the cattle had nothing to eat. Then the people of Egypt cried to Pharaoh for food, and the ruler said: "Go to Joseph, and do what he tells you."

The hungry, worried Egyptians came to the governor, and Joseph was prepared for their needs. He opened the huge storehouses and sold grain to all the people. Thus Joseph's years of hard work and planning were rewarded, and he saved the nation from starvation. There was food in Egypt; but in the land of Canaan where Jacob and his eleven sons lived, there was a great famine. Soon Jacob's family would be hungry if a way was not found to get food.

17

FOOD *for the* HUNGRY

GENESIS 42

ONE hot day when there had been no rain for many months, Jacob called his sons to his tent. The meadows were brown, the stalks of grain withered in the dust, and wide cracks appeared in the soil that was baked by the hot winds. Jacob and his sons knew that if the dry weather continued, the family would soon face famine. The men were tired and hot from their work, and the threat of hunger caused them to cast worried glances at one another. Where could they get food for their wives and their children?

Jacob spoke sharply to his sons. "Why do you stare at one another? I have just heard," he said, "that there is grain in Egypt; go down there, and buy some for us there, that we may live and not die."

At the word "Egypt" the ten brothers dropped their heads. They remembered that they had sold Joseph many years before to a caravan of traders heading for that land. Since that day the guilty men had not talked about Egypt. And now, as if to haunt them, their father was commanding them to go there to buy grain. Benjamin, the youngest brother, was not to make the journey, for Jacob was determined to protect the son of Rachel that he had left.

(209)

The ten brothers bowed before the royal officer, Joseph, whom they did not know.

V. WILKE, ARTIST

There was nothing the ten men could do but obey their father's command. Therefore they set out with their pack animals on the road that led over the hills and through the desert. They journeyed for days before they came to the great fortress that stood at the entrance to the land of Egypt. After the guards had inspected the travelers, they were allowed to pass into the country. They made their way along the highway to the capital city where throngs of people were going to buy grain from the governor. The ten brothers found their place in the crowd and awaited their turn. When their turn came they made their request for grain to the royal officer. Joseph recognized his brothers at once, but they did not dream that he was Joseph. He did not reveal his secret, but treated his brothers as strangers. He spoke to them in the language of Egypt, and his words were translated so they could understand them.

"Where have you come from?" he said to them.

"From the land of Canaan to buy food," they said.

Joseph remembered how his brothers had put him in the pit and later sold him as a slave. He wondered if they were as cruel and wicked as they had been twenty years before. To test them, he said: "You are spies; you have come to find out the condition of the land!"

But they denied this, saying: "Your servants are brothers, twelve in all; we are sons of a certain man in the land of Canaan; the youngest is at present with our father, while the other is no more." By their words they revealed that they had never been able to forget their missing brother, Joseph.

Acting like a stern governor, Joseph continued to accuse them of being spies. He said that the only way they could prove

Joseph went out into the fields and directed where the grain should be stored

© P. P. P. A., N. BRICE, ARTIST

that they were honest men was to send for their youngest brother. At a signal from Joseph, the Egyptian guard took the men to a dungeon, where they lay frightened and miserable.

At the end of three days Joseph called his brothers before him again. He had a plan to test them to see if they were now true to their father. He said: "Since I am one who fears God, you may save your lives, if you do this: if you are honest men, let one of you brothers remain confined in your prison and then the rest of you, go and take grain home to your starving households; but you must bring me your youngest brother. Thus shall your words be verified, and you shall not die."

The sons of Jacob talked among themselves in their own language after Joseph had spoken, and they did not know he could understand what they said. Reuben reminded them of how he had tried to save Joseph, but that they had carried out

Simeon was confined to the prison at the command of Joseph, but the rest of the brothers were allowed to take their grain and start for their father's home in Canaan.

W. WILKE, ARTIST

The nine sons of Jacob traveled along the highway leading from Egypt. On their journey they wondered how they would explain Simeon's imprisonment to their aged father.

their evil deed, and now this punishment was coming upon
them.

When Joseph spoke to his brothers again he commanded
that Simeon be put in prison. Then the nine men were given
bags of grain; but, unknown to them, Joseph ordered that their
money be placed in the top of their sacks. The sons of Jacob
loaded their pack animals and started toward Canaan. They
were silent and afraid because of what the governor had done,
and they wondered how they would explain Simeon's imprisonment to their father.

At the end of the day they stopped at a camping place, and
one of the brothers opened his sack to give his donkey some
grain. When he looked in the bag he gave a cry of surprise and

Jacob, old and lonely, sat in the door of his tent mourning the loss of his sons. He said sorrowfully: "Joseph is no more, Simeon is no more, and now you would take Benjamin."

distress. "My money has been put back! It is right here inside my sack!" he said to his brothers.

They were certain that this was a terrible mistake. They had been accused of being spies, and now here was proof that they were thieves. They hurried along on their homeward journey to tell their father what had happened.

In the door of Jacob's tent the nine sons gathered before the aged pioneer. They tried to tell what had happened, but their father could not understand why Simeon had been left in prison. They told their father that they must take Benjamin with them on the next trip to Egypt, but he would not listen. Then, to make matters worse, when the other men opened their bags, each one found his money in his sack. They had not paid for any of the grain that had been sold to them by the royal officer! Now terror filled their hearts. They never wanted to see Egypt again. All of this time Jacob was weeping for his lost son. He said: "It is I that you bereave. Joseph is no more, Simeon is no more, and now you would take Benjamin! It is on me that all this falls."

Reuben tried to reason with his father by saying that the governor would not see them if they did not bring Benjamin on the next trip. He promised that he would be responsible for the safety of the youngest son when they made the journey. But Jacob would not listen to his son's words. His words were firm: "My son shall not go down with you." And there the matter rested.

The nine sons left their father's tent and went to their wives and families. They were thankful to have food to eat, for the famine was severe. But as the brothers looked at the sacks of grain, they knew it would not be long until it would be necessary for them to go to Egypt again. "Egypt!" They hated the word more than ever before!

W. WILKE, ARTIST

The committee worked hard to make the Egyptian booth one of the show places of the annual school program. Captain Lane came to inspect the job Bette and Ruth were supervising.

The LAND of the PYRAMIDS

"OF COURSE, I like the idea, Bette. It's clever and different; but it will take a lot of planning and hard work to make it a success."

"I'm sure of that, too," admitted Bette; "but the committee voted to do it, Ruth, and if we all get behind it we can make it a success."

Bette Barrett and her chum, Ruth Gibson, talked as they ate their lunch in the school cafeteria during the noon hour.

"Here comes Roy now. Let's ask him what he thinks of the plan," suggested Bette. The girl smiled at her twin as he approached the table. She was as proud of her brothers, Roy and Dick, as any sister should be.

"What are you two so excited about?" asked the youth, sitting down in the vacant chair across the table from where the girls were eating their dessert of ice cream. "I was watching you while Dick and I ate our lunch. You never stopped talking for a minute."

"It's important, Roy," returned Bette. "We were planning the annual school program. The committee has decided to have a make-believe world fair. There will be booths with exhibits and students in costumes to represent different countries."

(217)

"And the program will be made up of music and other numbers from foreign lands," added Ruth Gibson. "We'll have China, Hawaii, Australia, Russia, India—"

"Don't forget Ireland and Egypt," put in Bette. "Our class is to have Egypt, Roy. What do you think of that?"

"Hm-m! Have you ever been there?" asked the boy with a roguish smile. Roy always enjoyed teasing his sister when she was especially serious.

"Don't be silly, Roy. We can do it. It's true, we may need some help," Bette admitted; "but it can be a success."

"Do you suppose Captain Lane would help us?" queried Ruth. "He's been to Egypt, and he could give us some good suggestions."

"He always co-operates 100 per cent in anything we ask him to do." The boy nodded his approval. "It wouldn't hurt to tell him about it, anyway. There goes the bell! Excuse me or I'll be late to manual arts class. If you need a mummy or if you want any brand-new pyramids built, send for me."

"Roy's a tease," Bette said as she smiled at Ruth. "But you can see he really likes the idea. I know he'll help."

"Suppose we stop by Captain Lane's house this afternoon on the way home from school," said Ruth. Bette agreed as she pushed back her chair and the two girls arose from the table. Ruth Gibson, six months younger than Bette, had been a close friend since the two girls had entered school in the first grade. Her dark brown eyes and brown hair offered a contrast to Bette's golden blond tresses and blue eyes. Since the Gibsons' house was only around the corner from the Barretts', the two were almost inseparable chums.

Captain Lane was digging bulbs in his flower bed when Bette and Ruth entered the garden gate. "We need some help in planning the annual school program," Bette said.

Captain Lane was digging bulbs in his flower beds when Bette and Ruth entered the garden gate later in the afternoon.

"Hello, girls!" called the man, waving his small spade in the air as a signal of welcome.

"Good afternoon, Captain Tim," returned Bette gaily. "You know Ruth, don't you?"

"Most assuredly I do." The captain flashed a jovial smile. "You've been out to Hillcrest Farm with us several times."

"That's right," Ruth said. "And one time there was plenty of excitement when the billy goat chased me."

"I remember that. Chips saved you from trouble by diverting

(Left) The Sphinx, centuries old, seems to stand guard near the Great Pyramid.

(Below) The ancient temple of Isis, a sacred spot for the Egyptians, who worshiped many gods.

© PUBLISHERS' P[HOTO]

(Above) Camel carav[an,] date palm trees, and pyramids are all com[mon] to the land of the N[ile.]

(Below) An ancient t[ablet,] written in hieroglyphics, [tell-] ing of a victory by on[e of] the conquering phara[ohs.]

© PUBLISHERS' PHOTO

Bricks are dried in the sun by the people of Egypt today in much the same way as they were made in Moses' time.

INTERNAT[IONAL]

the old fellow's attention." Captain Lane continued to dig bulbs as he talked. "What is on your mind this afternoon? I can see plans popping out of your eyes."

"We need some help in planning the annual school program, Captain Tim," Bette admitted, coming straight to the point.

"What's up now? I always buy tickets. Is that it?"

"Not this time, captain," Ruth chimed in quickly. "We need your brains, too."

"That is flattering." The man laughed as he spoke. "All right, I'll sit here on the wheelbarrow and you tell me about it. But wait a minute before you begin. Here comes someone."

"It's Roy," said Bette, turning around to see her twin brother entering the gate. The boy whistled merrily as he came up the garden path.

"Looks like I'm in time for the big council," he said as he came near.

"You can help us persuade Captain Lane," Ruth said.

"I'm a better listener. Bette got all the conversation ability when we were born. I'm the silent twin," the boy explained.

"No one would ever guess it, Roy," returned Bette in her own defense. "Anyway, here is the plan."

For the next five minutes the girls outlined the school program to their genial host, and finally Ruth said: "Now we want to know all about Egypt, for that is the country we must feature in our booth."

"We've been talking about the land of the Nile lately, haven't we, Roy?"

"Yes, Captain Tim, we were mentioning it in connection with the story of Joseph."

"That's right," said the man. "Dick has an essay to write on Egypt, and we are to hear it when he has it completed."

"What is the country like?" asked Bette.

"For one thing, there's desert on two sides—the east and the west. The Nile River has its beginning in the mountains far to the south and flows for some four thousand miles before reaching the Mediterranean Sea." Captain Lane drew a crude map on the ground with his spade to illustrate the geography of the country.

"Whenever I think of Egypt, I think of pyramids," Ruth Gibson declared. "I would like to see them sometime."

"There is an idea!" exclaimed Bette. "We could have pyramids painted or drawn on the background for our booth."

"You should have palm trees in the picture," suggested Roy, and then he teasingly said: "Perhaps you could have a mummy too."

"Can't you forget the mummy, Roy? I won't be there if we have one, that's certain. I don't like the thought of it."

Captain Lane smiled at Bette's emphatic words. There was a twinkle in his eye as he said: "I don't believe you'd have as many customers, Roy, as far as the girls are concerned."

"I guess you're right," agreed the youth. "But we can have palm trees, camels, and a pyramid in the picture. By the way, Captain Tim, did you ever climb to the top of one of the pyramids?"

"Don't get me started on that," begged the man, shaking his head. "I'll never forget that trip."

"Now you will have to tell us about it," said Bette.

"Yes, do," chimed in Ruth.

"I'll get through this story in a hurry," said the man, shaking his head. "It was a hot day, and the pyramids are on the edge of the desert. We arrived about ten o'clock in the morning at the Great Pyramid built by King Khufu, also named Cheops. It is the largest of the many pyramids found in Egypt. I think it was originally about 483 feet high, and about 755 feet on each side. But some of the stones have fallen off, and others have been weathered and broken by the passing centuries.

"There were native guides waiting when we arrived in the car, and I wondered what they would do to help us. I soon found out," the storyteller added.

"What did they do?" asked Roy.

"When I started clambering up the stones, I found two natives

Near the great pyramids of the Nile Valley one may today see the Mohammedans kneel beside their camels while they pray—a part of their worship that is centuries old.

GREEN, GENDREAU

waiting to pull me by the hands. And when they pulled, another fellow got behind me and pushed me up. How was that for service?"

"Did they do that for you all the way to the top?"

"Yes, all the way. And I needed the help, too, for the stones are about four feet high, weighing on an average of two and a half tons. When we reached the top we sat down on the stones and rested. I had my field glasses and camera with me, so I spent some time taking pictures and looking up and down the Nile River and at the city of Cairo a few miles away. But my muscles were stiff for several days after that climb."

"How were the pyramids built?" Roy asked thinking of the task it must have been to get the stones into their proper place high on the side of this monument.

"They were no doubt built by thousands of workmen, probably slaves. The rock was cut from a quarry up the Nile River and floated down on rafts to a place near the site of the pyramid. Then the stones were probably dragged up great inclines to their proper position. It must have been a stupendous job, for there were about 2,300,000 huge blocks of stone in the Great Pyramid."

"What were the pyramids—only monuments of stone?" queried Ruth.

"No," answered the captain. "They were tombs for the pharaohs. One of the first things a king would do when he came to the throne was to begin plans for his tomb. Some built pyramids, while others had their tombs carved out of solid rock in the sides of mountains. Many of these have been found in the Valley of the Tombs of the Kings at Thebes."

The splendor of the Pharaohs may be seen in the temples, the tombs, and the monuments of Egypt. The avenue of the sphinxes at Karnak is an example of their glory.

"Wasn't King Tut found in such a tomb?" asked Roy.

"You mean King Tutankhamen, I suppose. Yes, his wonderful tomb full of treasures was discovered in 1922. There was the king's furniture, beautifully carved, and jewels of many kinds. The archaeologists made one of the greatest discoveries of ancient Egypt when they found this tomb. The dishes, vases, chairs, and chests were more than three thousand years old. Some of the kings had pets of which they were very fond. Mummified monkeys and dogs have been found in the tombs of the pharaohs."

"What kind of clothes did the people wear in ancient times?" questioned Bette.

"In the time of Joseph the women wore shirts and a loose robe thrown over their shoulders. The men wore a kind of apron and a sort of shirt with sleeves," Captain Lane replied. "You would be interested in the fact that women who put color on their skin are not doing anything new today. The Egyptian women painted black circles around their eyes to make them look larger."

"Imagine that!" Ruth exclaimed. "I don't think we want to look like that in our program, Bette!"

"No, hardly," agreed Bette. "I wonder how the women looked at themselves. I read somewhere that glass mirrors were not invented until modern times."

"They looked at themselves, you may be sure," the man said with a hearty laugh. "Mirrors of polished copper have been found in the tombs, and these must have made quite good mirrors. By the way, boys wore their heads shaved except for a long strand of hair on the right side. That was braided into a pigtail, the sign of boyhood. When they grew to manhood their heads were shaved completely."

"I remember the Bible tells how Joseph shaved himself before he went to the palace to see Pharaoh," suggested Roy.

"Did you ever try to imagine what young Joseph must have thought when he reached Egypt where there were so many idols?" The captain put the question to his three listeners.

"It must have been strange to him, even as it would be for us to be dropped suddenly into China or India," Roy responded.

"What kind of gods did they worship?" Bette plied her question to get another story from her friend.

"They worshiped almost everything—baboons, cats, cows,

and bulls. The hippopotamus and crocodile in the river were gods. They kept snakes in their houses as sacred creatures."

"That's when I would have left," said Ruth emphatically.

"I'd be one jump ahead of you, Ruth," Bette added.

"In such a heathen land it must have been a brave thing for Joseph to tell Pharaoh about the true God," Captain Lane continued. "I've always admired his courage when he told Pharaoh the meaning of his dreams."

"What's going on here?" A voice broke in suddenly, and the captain and his three young friends turned toward the gate. There stood Dick, football in hand.

"We're making plans for the school program and talking about Egypt," Bette said quickly. "Come and join us."

"I'm going to the park to kick my football for a while. I was looking for you, Roy. Aren't you coming with me?"

Ancient methods of plowing the land and threshing the grain may still be seen in the shadow of the pyramids. The Egyptian is threshing grain with a sled drawn by oxen.

"Of course, Dick. But wait a few minutes until we finish this story. Captain Lane told us about climbing the Great Pyramid."

"Say, I'm really missing something." Dick came up on the run and whirled his brother off the box on which he had been sitting. There was a mad scramble which ended in the brothers' sharing the seat, which was rather narrow for two husky boys.

"What have you found out about Egypt for your essay?" began the captain, when his friends had settled down to hear the rest of the story.

"I haven't had much time yet," Dick returned. "But I did find out how the Nile River helps the country. It seems that the river begins to rise about the middle of June when the melting snows of the mountains bring the water down to the lowlands. In that season the river turns from green to dark red."

"Why is that?" Ruth asked.

"That's because there is so much red soil in the water when it is at flood tide. Then as the floodwaters begin to drop, some of that soil is left behind on the farms of Egypt. The men begin plowing as soon as the water drains off the land, and then they plant their seed."

"Good work, Dick," said the captain. "To know about the Nile River is important, for the land has depended on it for thousands of years for its crops. The river must have failed to rise during the seven years of famine when Joseph was in Pharaoh's court."

"Did the people live in houses?" asked Bette.

"Yes, we know that the better homes were made of brick. Many of them had two stories, and on the top was a roof garden,

Primitive methods are still employed to draw water from the river for irrigation.

where the family would spend the warm evenings. The floors
of the houses were of stone or clay."

"Probably Joseph lived in such a house with his wife and two
sons," suggested Roy. "I wonder if Ephraim and Manasseh had
toys when they were little?"

"They probably did," said Captain Lane. "Some of the toys
of that time have been found. One of them was a wooden cat
with glass eyes and a movable lower jaw."

"They were boys and girls like us, I suppose," Bette added.
"I imagine the little girls had dolls of some sort to play with."

"I found out that the men loved to hunt," Dick spoke up
from his perch on the box. "The men hunted the gazelle in the
hills, and on the river they caught the crocodile and hippopotamus. That must have been a dangerous sport."

"They didn't have guns, either," Roy reminded his brother.

"I must be going, Roy. If you're going to kick this football,
too, you'll have to come with me now."

"You'll excuse us, Captain Lane," said Roy, as the brothers
arose to leave.

"Indeed, I will. In fact," the man continued, "I think we've
suggested about everything we can for these girls. They should
have some ideas for their program now."

"Thank you, captain," said Bette. "This has been a big help.
I thought of one thing more. You know that Joseph rode in a
chariot. Well, I wish we could make something like that for
our booth."

"Get the boys to help you," the man suggested. "They always
like to work with tools. You'll find some pictures of Egypt in a
book in my library. I think there are pictures of chariots and also

of the costumes of the Egyptians. If you'll come over this evening when I'm through digging up bulbs, I'll show it to you."

The girls were standing at the garden gate, and Bette called
back: "We'll be over for a few minutes. I want to finish the story
of Joseph tonight. I'm anxious to find out what happened to
him and his brothers in Egypt. I'm afraid we have bothered you
too long now. Good-by!"

They were gone. The captain turned the bulbs out of rich
soil and placed them in the box. "Bother?" he said to himself.
"If they didn't come to see me, I'd have been an old fossil long
ago. Maybe I am anyway, I tell so many stories about what I've
done and where I've been. Hm-m! But it's fun; yes, sir, it's fun,
just the same. And do they help keep me young!"

18

JOSEPH FACES His BROTHERS

GENESIS 43 to 45:24

NO RAIN fell in the land of Canaan, and the famine dragged on month after month. Jacob was thankful for the supply of food that his sons had brought from Egypt. But every time the nine brothers went to get grain from the sacks, they thought of Simeon in prison in that faraway land. The food supply was dwindling fast, and they knew they should soon start on another trip to Egypt. But they did not dare to talk about it to their father, for what would he say if they asked him to allow Benjamin to go with them?

The day came, however, when Jacob was forced to call his sons to his tent. "Go again, and buy us a little food," he commanded.

But Judah said to him: "The man strictly warned us: 'You cannot have audience with me unless your brother is with you.'"

The aged pioneer knew that Benjamin must go on the dangerous journey, but he bowed his head while Judah was speaking. "Let the lad go with me," said Judah to his father Israel; "but we must go at once, if we would save our lives and not die, both we, you, and our dependents."

Jacob finally agreed, saying: "If it must be so, then do this." He instructed his sons to take presents to the officer in Egypt,

(233)

The brothers were placed at a large banquet table, while Joseph ate his meal alone.

W. WILKE, ARTIST

Joseph saw Benjamin and he asked the brothers: "Is this your youngest brother of whom you told me?" They assured him that this was Benjamin, the son dear to their father.

presents of honey, nuts, spices, and myrrh. They were also to take double money to repay that which had been found in their sacks as well as to buy more grain. Then the father gave a final word of blessing, praying God to care for them on their dangerous mission. He said: "Take your brother too, and go, return to the man. May God Almighty grant you such kindness with the man that he will release your other brother for you, as well as Benjamin."

The brothers made the journey to Egypt in good time, and again they were brought before Joseph, the royal officer in charge of selling grain. When he saw Benjamin with his brothers, he commanded his servant to take the men to his home and prepare a dinner for them. He would give them only the best food.

Fear came to their hearts, however, when they saw that they were being taken to the royal officer's home. Would he punish them because of the money they had unknowingly taken in their sacks? When they arrived at the house, the brothers spoke at once to the chief steward who welcomed them at the door.

"If you please, sir," they said, "we came down the first time specially to buy food, but when we reached the camping place for the night, and opened our sacks, there was each man's money in the mouth of his sack—our money in full. Accordingly we have brought it back with us, and we have brought other money down with us to buy food. We do not know who put our money in our sacks."

The steward answered them kindly and told them not to be afraid. Soon Simeon was brought in, and there was a happy re-union with the brother who had been held in prison. They were amazed that they should be honored in the governor's home.

Judah pleaded with his father to allow Benjamin to make the trip to Egypt. At last Jacob agreed, and he sent presents of honey, nuts, spices, and myrrh to the royal officer.
W. WILKE, ARTIST

When Joseph arrived, the brothers hurried to get their presents. Bowing low before the governor, they gave him the gifts from their father Jacob. Joseph was anxious to know about his father's health. "Is your father well," he said, "the old man of whom you spoke? Is he still living?"

"Your servant, our father, is well; he is still living," they said, bowing in homage to him. Joseph must have thought of his boyhood dreams when the brothers' sheaves and the sun, moon, and eleven stars bowed before him. But as yet he would not tell them who he was, for he wanted to test them further to see if there was love in their hearts—such love as they had not known when they sold him as a slave. Looking at Benjamin, he asked: "Is this your youngest brother, of whom you told me?" And they assured him that it was.

The dinner was served, and the brothers were placed at one large table. Joseph ate at a table by himself, since it was not the

The travelers had gone only a few miles on their homeward journey when Joseph's steward stopped them. After careful search the cup was found in Benjamin's sack.

W. WILKE, ARTIST

custom for Egyptians to eat with foreigners. The eleven sons
of Jacob were seated according to their age, from the oldest to
the youngest. They were amazed that the governor should know
the order of their birth. The men had another surprise coming,
for while they ate they noticed that Benjamin was given five
times as much food and drink as they received.

Now Joseph had given a special command to his steward
concerning the bags of grain. He told them to fill the sacks and
put each man's money in the top of his sack. In Benjamin's sack
he was also to put Joseph's silver cup.

Early the next morning the travelers set out on their journey
toward home. They were indeed happy, for all eleven of them
were returning to their father. But they had gone only a few
miles when Joseph's steward came riding furiously after them
and stopped them on the road. He accused them of stealing the
governor's silver cup.

The brothers declared that they were innocent of the charge.
They said that the one in whose possession the cup was found
should become a slave for life. To prove it, each one unloaded
his sack and opened it for inspection. The steward began his
search with Reuben, the oldest son, and went on down the line,
according to their ages. When the steward came to Benjamin's
sack, he found the beautiful silver cup! The brothers were
struck with grief and terror. They tore their garments and cried
aloud. What could they do to save Benjamin? How would
they answer their father for another lost son?

Sick at heart, the men returned to the city and stood once
more before the governor. "What is this that you have done?"
Joseph said to them.

A dreadful silence fell on the men for a moment, and then Judah stepped forward and said: "What can we say to my lord? What can we urge? How can we prove our innocence? God has discovered the crime of your servants; here we are, the slaves of my lord, both we and he in whose possession the cup has been found."

Joseph explained that it was only the man in whose sack the cup had been found that would be his slave for life. He added: "The rest of you are free to go back to your father."

Go to their father! Again the thought brought fear to the sons of Jacob. They knew how he had mourned years before when he learned that Joseph was gone. Now he was feeble, and the news that Benjamin was a slave would surely cause the old man's death.

Judah then told the governor of Jacob's love for his youngest son. He revealed his father's sorrow at having to say good-by to Benjamin when they started on the trip. As Judah spoke, Joseph saw that a wonderful change had taken place in the hearts of his brothers. They were not the same cruel, evil men who had sold him to the traders. As a final plea, Judah said: "Now then, pray let your servant remain in the boy's place as my lord's slave, but let the boy go back with his brothers; for how can I go back to my father unless the boy is with me, and witness the agony that would come to my father?"

When Joseph saw Judah's love for his father and for Benjamin he could no longer hide himself from his brothers. He commanded all the officials to leave the room, and then, stretching forth his hands, he said: "I am Joseph. Is my father still living?"

Joseph stood up and said to his brothers: "I am Joseph. Is my father still living?"

W. WILKE, ARTIST

All of the longing for home came back to the long-lost son in that moment. For twenty years he had been in a foreign country; now the dream of seeing his father might come true!

The brothers stood in dumb amazement before him. They could not speak, so great was their astonishment. Joseph, their lost brother, a ruler in Egypt! They were afraid when they thought of their guilt and realized that Joseph could take his revenge. In a flash Joseph realized how they felt, and he said: "Come nearer to me."

When they were close to him, he said: "I am your brother Joseph whom you sold into Egypt. Now do not be distressed nor angry with yourselves that you sold me here; for it was to save a life that God sent me ahead of you; for it is two years now that the famine has prevailed in the land, but there are still five years in which there will be no plowing or reaping. God sent

Soon the eleven brothers were on their way home once more. This time they had wagons that were loaded with precious gifts from Joseph for his aged father Jacob.

W. WILKE, ARTIST

me ahead of you to ensure you a remnant in the earth, and to be the means of a remarkable escape for you."

The brothers could scarcely believe what they heard. Joseph was forgiving them! He kissed them and spoke words of peace and comfort to them. Then they talked of all the things that had happened during the years Joseph had been absent from home.

The news that Joseph's brothers had arrived was told to Pharaoh, and he welcomed them, saying: "I will give you the best of the land of Egypt." He invited them to move their families and their father to his country so that they could enjoy its riches.

Soon the eleven brothers were on their way home once more. This time they had wagons to bring all their goods back to Egypt, and they carried precious gifts. They remembered Joseph's message to his father, how he had told them to say: "Since God has made me lord of all Egypt, come down to me without delay. You shall live in the land of Goshen, and be near me, you, your sons, your grandsons, your flocks, your herds, and all that belong to you."

As the eleven sons made their way across the desert, they wondered if Jacob would believe them when they told him Joseph was alive. Now they must tell their father how they had sold Joseph and how they had lied and deceived him years before. It would not be easy to reveal all of this to Jacob and to ask him to forgive them.

19

FATHER and SON MEET

GENESIS 45:25 to 47:31

JACOB anxiously waited at Hebron for the return of his sons. For him the days passed slowly, and he sent his servants out many times to watch for the travelers. At last the day came when a servant came running to tell him that his sons were coming. He left his tent and stood watching them coming across the field. He counted the boys when they were near enough to be seen. There were ten, eleven; yes, eleven! There were smiles on their faces, too. Evidently they had been successful on their journey.

The brothers came on ahead of the caravan, and Jacob saw that they were excited about something. They all began to speak at once. "Joseph is still living, and he is ruler over all the land of Egypt," they told him.

"Joseph"—"ruler"—"Egypt." The words stunned the aged pioneer, and he could not understand what his sons were talking about. They repeated the words over and over. They told him how they had sold Joseph years before, and they asked him to forgive them for their evil deed. Then they brought the presents that Joseph had sent, and they showed him the wagons that were to take him and all his possessions to their new home in the land of the Nile.

(243)

It was a glad reunion when the long-lost son welcomed his father's family to Egypt.

GRAMSTORFF BROS., H. SCHOPIN, ARTIST

Old people do not usually like to leave home; but when Jacob realized that Joseph was actually alive he was ready to go. "Enough!" said Israel; "my son Joseph is still living; I will go and see him before I die."

God sent the faithful pioneer a message of courage. In a dream Jacob was told not to be afraid to go to the land of Egypt, for his children would prosper and become a great nation. And, best of all, they would come back again to Canaan.

Soon the baggage was loaded, and the family set out on their journey. There were sixty-six members of Jacob's family, including the sons' wives and children, in the caravan. Joseph, his wife, and their two children, made four more members of the family, so there were seventy people in Jacob's family when he arrived in Egypt.

When the caravan came to the frontier fortress, the guard allowed it to pass through at once, for the soldiers had been told that the governor's family was coming to live in Egypt. On the wagons rolled until they reached the land of Goshen. Joseph's messengers told him when the caravan was arriving, and he rode in his chariot to meet his father. It was a glad reunion when the long-lost son threw his arms around his aged father.

"Now at last I may die," Israel said to Joseph, "after having seen from your very self that you are still alive."

Jacob and his sons made their home in the land of Goshen, a rich and well-watered part of Egypt. When Pharaoh heard that Joseph's family had arrived, he was anxious to meet Jacob. The momentous day came when the brave pioneer and five of his sons were brought to the king's palace. There Jacob saw the magnificent building, the gold throne, the soldiers and courtiers.

He realized the greatness of Egypt, and he was proud that his son was governor, next to Pharaoh himself.

"How old are you?" Pharaoh said to Jacob.

"The length of my life as an immigrant has been one hundred and thirty years," Jacob said to Pharaoh; "few and hard have been the years of my life." No doubt the man of God remembered some of the hardships—the flight from his home after he had cheated Esau, his years of work in Haran, the death of his dearest wife, and the loss of Joseph. But in spite of all this, Jacob counted his blessings. God had promised to make his children a strong nation.

Joseph was a busy man, for the famine continued year after year. But, first of all, he saw that his family had plenty of food and supplies in their new home. After the famine was over, Joseph continued his duties as a royal officer. The sons of Jacob prospered in Egypt, and the family grew. But as the years passed, Jacob grew feeble and was nearing the end of his life. He sent for Joseph to come to his bedside and requested that his son promise that he would bury his father in the Cave of Machpelah, where Abraham and the other members of the family had been buried. Joseph promised that he would fulfill his father's request.

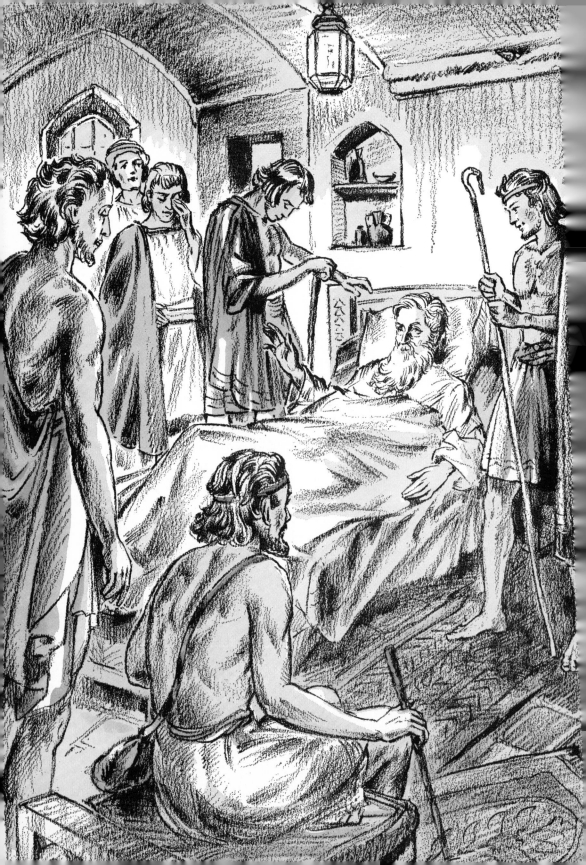

20

UNDER *a* CRUEL KING

GENESIS 48 to 50

WHEN Jacob knew that he was about to die, he called his sons and Joseph's two sons to him and gave them each a special blessing. He told them how the Lord had been with him in all the years of his life, and he repeated the promises that the family should become a great nation.

When the father died, there was mourning in the land for seventy days. Joseph had the body embalmed according to the custom of the Egyptians. After the days of mourning, Joseph asked Pharaoh for permission to go to his old home and bury his father in the Cave of Machpelah. The king readily granted the request, and a large funeral procession made the journey to Canaan. In it were the family of Jacob, the king's courtiers, and companies of soldiers on horseback.

Returning to Egypt after the burial of their father, the sons were afraid that Joseph might seek revenge on them for the way they had treated him years before. They thought he might have been waiting until his father died before punishing them. Therefore they came to Joseph and again asked his forgiveness.

Joseph said to them: "Do not be afraid; for can I take God's place? You meant to do me harm, but God accounted it good, in order to do as He has done today: save the lives of many peo-

(247)

Jacob summoned his twelve sons to his bedside and gave a blessing to each one.

W. WILKE, ARTIST

ple. So now, do not be afraid; I myself will provide for you and your dependents."

Joseph did not hate his brothers or try to "get even" with them for the way they had treated him. He saw how God had guided his life and had been with them through the years.

The brothers were happy at this assurance from Joseph, and the family prospered as the years passed. As long as Joseph lived, his brothers were honored in Egypt. When he was one hundred ten years old he knew he was about to die, so he called his brothers and said to them: "I am about to die; but God will be sure to take note of you, and take you up out of this land to the land which He promised on oath to Abraham, Isaac, and Jacob."

After Joseph's death other pharaohs came to the throne of Egypt, but they did not know of his fame and what he had done in saving the nation from famine. A pharaoh came to rule who saw that the family of Jacob was prospering in the land of Goshen. Because he was afraid they might become more powerful than the Egyptians, he made harsh laws against them. No longer were they free to dwell on their farms and raise cattle and sheep. Now they must work as slaves for the king.

The powerful pharaoh planned great new cities. He ordered thousands of laborers to work building these cities for him. Some of the workmen were the children of Jacob. In great gangs they were driven to work making bricks and carrying them to the builders. They worked from sunrise until dark, and there seemed no end to the work. In the time of cruel slavery they remembered the promise that had been made to Abraham, to Isaac, and to Jacob. They longed for the freedom of the land of Canaan where their fathers had lived.

God had not forgotten His promise. There would come a day when the children of Israel would be free and would return to their home in Canaan. The deliverance of the people would become one of the greatest stories of all time. The pioneers had blazed the trail to the land of Canaan, but someday faithful men, who would be the conquerors of the land, would lead the people to their promised home.

Captain Tim's Bible Quiz

"You have been asking me so many questions about the Bible," said Captain Tim to Bette Barrett one day, "I think it's time for me to ask you a few more. Here is a list of twenty questions about the story of Joseph. They cover the Bible story in Genesis from chapters 35 to 50."

Bette missed one question. How well can you do on this quiz? The answers are on page 252.

1. How old was Joseph when he had his two dreams?
2. What did Pharaoh see in his two dreams?
3. Which of the ten brothers did not want to kill Joseph?
4. What did the brothers find in their sacks of grain when they returned home after their first trip to Egypt?
5. What were the names of Joseph's two sons?
6. What did Pharaoh give Joseph after he had told the king the meaning of his dreams?
7. In what part of Egypt did Jacob and his sons live?
8. What special gift did Jacob give to Joseph when he was a boy?
9. What did Joseph send his father to carry the family to Egypt?
10. At the feast how much more food did Joseph give Benjamin than was given to any of the other brothers?
11. Who were the two men who had dreams in the prison?
12. For how much money did the brothers sell Joseph?
13. In whose sack was the silver cup of the governor found?
14. Which one of the brothers was left as a prisoner while the other sons returned home after their first trip to Egypt?
15. Who was Asenath?
16. How many persons were in Jacob's family when he went to Egypt, including Joseph and his wife and sons?
17. How many years of good crops preceded the famine?
18. Who did Joseph say was able to give the answer to Pharaoh's dreams?
19. Who was the mother of Joseph and Benjamin?
20. How did Joseph's dreams come true?

(250)

Answers to Bible Quiz

NUMBER I, PAGE 85

The correct answer, the Bible reference, and the page in this book where the facts are found (if they are stated in this book) are listed below.

1. Jared. Genesis 5:18.
2. Light. Genesis 1:3-5. Page 44.
3. Eight. Genesis 6:18. Page 73.
4. Cain. Genesis 4:1. Page 64.
5. Methuselah. Genesis 5:27. Page 71.
6. About twenty feet (fifteen cubits). Genesis 7:20. Page 75.
7. Sun, moon, and stars. Genesis 1:16-19. Page 47.
8. By water that came up out of the earth. Genesis 2:5, 6. Page 72.
9. An olive leaf. Genesis 8:10, 11. Page 76.
10. Enoch. Genesis 5:24. Page 71.
11. Mount Ararat. Genesis 8:4.
12. Cain. Genesis 4:9. Page 67.
13. Six hundred feet long, sixty feet high. Genesis 6:15. Page 71.
14. Adam. Genesis 2:20. Page 52.
15. The serpent. Genesis 3:4, 5. Page 57.
16. So that no sinful man could eat of the tree of life and thus live forever. Genesis 3:22-24. Page 62.
17. The seventh day. Genesis 2:1-3. Page 53.
18. Four rivers. Genesis 2:10.
19. Tree of the knowledge of good and evil. Genesis 2:16, 17. Page 56.
20. A lamb of his flock. Genesis 4:4. Page 65.

NUMBER II, PAGE 173

The correct answer, the Bible reference, and the page in this book where the facts are found (if they are stated in this book) are listed below.

1. Nimrod. Genesis 10:8, 9. Page 81.
2. Sarah. Genesis 21:3. Page 114.
3. In Babel on the plain of Shinar. Genesis 11:2, 9. Page 82.
4. Sodom and Gomorrah. Genesis 13:10, 11. Page 100.
5. Hagar. Genesis 16:15. Page 114.
6. A ram. Genesis 22:13. Page 121.
7. Seven years. Genesis 29:20. Page 160.
8. Jacob. Genesis 28:11. Page 155.
9. Jacob and Esau. Genesis 25:24-26. Page 147.

10. Only three. Genesis 19:30. Page 111.

11. Confused their language. Genesis 11:6, 7. Page 83.

12. Jacob. Genesis 32:24-27. Page 168.

13. Haran, where Nahor lived. Genesis 24:10. Page 125.

14. Lot's wife. Genesis 19:26. Page 110.

15. Four hundred. Genesis 33:1. Page 167.

16. Israel. Genesis 32:28. Page 168.

17. Isaac. Genesis 24:62-64. Page 131.

18. Egypt. Genesis 12:10. Page 99.

19. Lot and his family. Genesis 14:12. Page 100.

20. Two angels. Genesis 19:1, 15. Page 109.

—————————— NUMBER III, PAGE 250 ——————————

The correct answer, the Bible reference, and the page in this book where the facts are found (if they are stated in this book) are listed below.

1. Seventeen years old. Genesis 37:2-8. Page 188.

2. Seven fat cows, seven lean cows that ate the fat ones. Also seven full ears of grain and the seven thin ears that ate the full ears. Genesis 41:1-7. Pages 203, 204.

3. Reuben. Genesis 37:21. Page 190.

4. The money they had paid for the grain. Genesis 42:25, 35. Page 214.

5. Manasseh and Ephraim. Genesis 41:51, 52. Page 207.

6. His ring, beautiful clothes, a gold necklace, and a chariot. Genesis 41:42, 43. Page 206.

7. The land of Goshen. Genesis 47:6, 27. Page 244.

8. A coat of many colors. Genesis 37:3. Page 188.

9. Wagons. Genesis 45:27. Page 243.

10. Five times as much as to the other brothers. Genesis 43:34. Page 237.

11. Pharaoh's butler and baker. Genesis 40:1-5. Page 197.

12. Twenty pieces of silver. Genesis 37:28. Page 192.

13. Benjamin's sack. Genesis 44:12. Page 237.

14. Simeon. Genesis 42:24. Page 213.

15. The wife of Joseph. Genesis 41:45. Page 207.

16. Seventy. Genesis 46:26, 27. Page 244.

17. Seven years. Genesis 41:53. Page 206.

18. The God of heaven. Genesis 41:16. Page 203.

19. Rachel. Genesis 35:24. Page 187.

20. His brothers bowed before him when he was governor of Egypt. Genesis 43:26; 44:14. Page 236.